Fragments That Remain

Other Books by Amy Carmichael

Amy Carmichael of Dohnavur .... Biography by Frank L. Houghton

Candles in the Dark .... Letters of counsel

Edges of His Ways .... Daily devotional

Figures of the True .... Readings with photographs

God's Missionary .... Booklet on being a missionary

Gold by Moonlight .... Thoughts by A.C. with photographs

Gold Cord .... The story of *The Dohnavur Fellowship*

His Thoughts Said . . . His Father Said . . . . Short readings

If .... Challenging free verse beginning with *"If"*

Kohila .... A true story of an Indian woman

Learning of God .... Selected prose and poetry

Mimosa .... A true story of an Indian woman

Mountain Breezes .... Anthology of A.C.'s poetry

Rose From Brier .... Devotional, especially for the ill

Thou Givest . . . They Gather .... Topical devotional

Toward Jerusalem .... Selected poetry

Whispers of His Power .... Daily devotional

COMPILED BY BEE TREHANE
From the Notes and Letters of

Amy Carmichael

Fragments That Remain

PUBLICATIONS

Fort Washington, PA 19034

• *Fragments That Remain* •

Published by CLC ⋄ Publications

U.S.A.
P.O. Box 1449, Fort Washington, PA 19034

GREAT BRITAIN
51 The Dean, Alresford, Hants. SO24 9BJ

AUSTRALIA
P.O. Box 2299, Strathpine, QLD 4500

NEW ZEALAND
10 MacArthur Street, Feilding

ISBN 978-0-87508-972-0

Text set in *Garamond*

This printing 2007

Contents

Note on Bible Translations • vii

Prologue • ix

Basket 1 • Evangelism • 1

Basket 2 • Service • 15

Basket 3 • The Bible and First Principles • 31

Basket 4 • Prayer and Provision • 53

Basket 5 • Praise, Not Depression • 71

Basket 6 • Healing • 85

Basket 7 • Witness, Conflict and Victory • 109

Basket 8 • The Cross and Commitment • 123

Basket 9 • Walk in the Spirit • 137

Basket 10 • Guidance and Goads • 161

Basket 11 • En Route for Heaven • 179

Basket 12 • Triumph! • 191

Epilogue • 201

Acknowledgments

Bible quotations marked (NIV) are from the *New International Version.* Copyright © 1973, 1978, 1984 International Bible Society.

Quotations marked (GNB) are taken from the *Good News Bible,* copyright © American Bible Society 1976.

Extracts marked (BCP) are taken from *The Book of Common Prayer,* Crown Copyright in the United Kingdom, reproduced by permission of Eyre & Spottiswoode (Publishers) Limited, Her Majesty's Printers, London.

Quotations marked (NKJV) are from the *New King James version,* copyright © 1979, 1980, 1982 by Thomas Nelson, Inc.

All are used by permission.

Note on Bible Translations

Amy Carmichael was steeped in the language of the Author-ized King James Version of the Bible, but she loved other translations and paraphrases. Those she quotes in this book include: Coverdale's version of the Psalms in the *Book of Common Prayer* (BCP); Cheyne (*The Psalms*); W. J. Conybeare (*The Epistles of St. Paul*); J. N. Darby's version of the Bible; F. Delitzsch (*Notes on the Psalms*); W. Kay (*The Psalms*); J. B. Rotherham (*The Emphasized Bible*); the *Revised Version* of 1881; A. Way (*The Letters of St. Paul*); R. F. Weymouth (*The New Testament in Modern Speech*); and R. Young (*A Literal Translation of the Bible*).

I had the privilege of reading and commenting on the manuscripts of some of her last books, and she was always eager to accept suggestions and corrections, especially those which would make her message clearer. I believe that, had she lived to see them, she would have wished to use one of the modern versions of the Bible, more easily understood by the present generation. I have therefore taken the liberty in many places of changing the original King James Version to the *New* King James (NKJV), thus eliminating the use of "thee" and "thou," and the obsolete verb endings. To those who miss the cadences of the old, I offer my apologies.

Bee Trehane

Prologue

Amy Carmichael, whose writings have challenged and blessed thousands in many lands, was a down-to-earth mystic. Her intimate personal relationship with God as her Father, the Lord Jesus Christ as her beloved Savior and Friend, and the Holy Spirit as her constant Indweller and Enabler, was translated into everyday living in total commitment and unwavering trust.

Her missionary life began in 1893 in Japan. She writes: "In my room in Japan I had two words written on the wall: *Yes, Lord.*"

Those two words sum up her life and her teaching. "If to all our Lord asks of us—obedience, confidence in His love, guidance, purposes—we answer instantly, *Yes, Lord*, then there is nothing to hinder Him from using for our relief and help those eternal forces that are at His command. Limitless power is ours to use if we only know how, and if there is nothing in us to prevent its flow."

Thirty-six of her books were published during her lifetime. Since her death in 1951 in Dohnavur, South India, a further four books have been compiled from her letters, and from private notes never intended for publication. This fifth book is an attempt to "Gather up the fragments that remain, that nothing be lost," according to our Lord's command to His disciples after He had fed the five thousand with just five barley loaves and two fishes.

Although the fragments do indeed fill twelve "baskets," they are "broken pieces" scattered far and wide, covering many years and many experiences. It is impossible to fit them together into tidy loaves. Instead, this is an attempt to let Amy do what she herself liked to do: "More and more I feel unable for anything except just the telling of what this amazing Lord of ours does in and out of the common day. My mind runs that way. I like stories of people much better than good books by people. So it is a great comfort to me that the Lord took the boy's small fishes—a sardine sort of thing, the mere relish of the dish—and did not ask, for example, for salmon."

Here, then, are the broken pieces and the sardines; twelve "baskets" of "fragments that remain" from the life and work of Amy Carmichael.

Basket

1

Evangelism

❖ Today there is one full-time Christian worker for every 1500 of the population in the United Kingdom but only one for every two and three quarter *million* in Asia. The situation was no better when Amy first went to Japan in 1893, and the sight of millions who had never heard of the true God stirred her to the depths of her soul. She felt keenly her inability to speak Japanese.

In Japan

Think how you would feel if you were standing upon a rock around which were seething billows wherein were sinking and drowning men and women within your reach—yet just out of it. You safe, yet helpless to save them, helpless to stretch out a hand or throw a lifeline. Can you realize what it is to be plunged into silence just when your whole soul is longing most burningly to tell the good news you have come so far to bring?

The very sunshine seems sad, as, for the first time for me, it falls upon a figure worshiping—what? There he kneels, bowing till his forehead touches the ground, praying again and again, "but there was no voice, nor any that answered" (1 Kings 18:26).

In silence we watch him turn away half wistfully. None of us can speak, but we give him a Japanese copy of Luke 15 and he passes down the long avenue reading it.

❖ As soon as she had learned a little Japanese, Amy was out in the villages with a Christian interpreter, preaching and teaching and loving the people. She did not always get a friendly welcome.

Stoning

Tonight they pelted us as we were coming home. The stones were coming from all quarters at once. In the midst of it came the old psalm, "He shall cover you with His feathers, and under His wings you shall take refuge" (91:4, NKJV) and every fear seemed chased away. "Under His wings"—how real it seems when one is surrounded by a crowd of men and boys shouting and pressing, and our lantern only shows us faces angry and derisive. We were kept from any real harm, for He did take care of us—we knew He would.

How very real the Bible becomes to one in a heathen land. The story of the crowd that stoned Stephen for instance—one remembers how a Paul came out of it, and hope and courage to believe for another Paul come with the thought.

Then the promises are so infinitely more living than ever before. One has so many more chances of definitely proving them. And His presence is sometimes almost as literally felt as one feels the presence of another in the room. At home there was not so much room left for His all-satisfyingness, at least one wasn't so thrown back on Him for everything. Here it is Christ or *nothing*.

A Japanese village

We are going soon to a little village near here. They sent a beseeching letter: "We have only heard *once*, please do come and tell us more." Only heard once—think of what it means! And in every English village, how often have they heard? Oh the need, the pitiful need; how it wrings one's heart! I often wonder, would not the blessing at home be greater if instead of keeping your best, you sent them out to the regions beyond?

❖ Although she said she would never urge anyone to go to the mission field, her early letters from Japan, and then from Ceylon where she did village evangelism for a few months, are full of pleas.

The Cost

I would never urge one to come to the heathen unless he felt the burden for souls and the Master's call; but oh, I wonder so few do! It does cost something. Satan is tenfold more of a reality to me today than he was in England, and very keenly that awful home-longing cuts through and through one some-times—but there is a strange deep joy in being here with Jesus.

Praising helps more than anything. Sometimes one wakens with the feeling of "miss"—indescribable except to those who know it—and the temptation is to give way and go in for a regular spell of homesickness and be no good to anybody. *Then* you feel the home prayers; they help you to begin straight off and sing "Glory, glory, Hallelujah," and you find your cup is ready to overflow again after all.

The Unequal Distribution

The front rows of the Five Thousand are getting the loaves and the fishes over and over again—till it seems as though they have to be bribed and besought to accept them—while the back rows are almost forgotten. Is it that we are so busy with the front rows, which we can see, that we have no time for the back rows out of sight? But is it fair? Is it what Jesus our Master intends? *Can* this unequal distribution of the Bread of Life really be called fair?

Could you say to a heathen woman, "I am very sorry for you. I know this will not show you the way from the dark where you are to the light where I am. To show you the way I must go to you, or send someone whom I want for myself, or do without something which I wish to have. And this of course is impossible. It might be done if I loved God enough. But I love myself more than God or you."

You would not say such a thing. But—"Whoever has this world's goods, and sees his brother in need, and shuts up his heart from him, how does the love of God abide in him?" (1 John 3:17, NKJV).

Our Responsibility

"Deliver those who are drawn towards death, and hold back those stumbling to the slaughter. If you say, 'Surely we did not know this,' does not He who weighs the hearts consider it? He who keeps your soul, does He not know it? And will He not render to each man according to his deeds?" (Prov. 24:11–12, NKJV).

"And he called ten servants of his, and gave them ten pounds, and said unto them, Trade ye herewith till I come" (Luke 19:13, RV).

Till He come, let us trade. *Are* we trading? Are we in earnest, or do we dream that we are? Asleep and dreaming, busy dreams but dreaming still, playing with life's realities, playing prettily perhaps, but playing still.

Oh! Don't let us dream through the "little while" (till He comes), don't let us toy with eternity.

❖ From Japan to Ceylon to India Amy went, always confident of the Lord's guidance and direction. Her first five years in India were spent in itinerant village evangelism with a band of Indian Christian women whom she led and trained. She learned the difficult Tamil language of South India so well that, in the dark, she could pass for an Indian. She learned the ways and thoughts of the Indian people, and the more she learned the more deeply she loved them and longed for their salvation. Her letters home still urged upon her readers the desperate need of the unreached.

Evangelization

The evangelization of the world is a great word, but boil it down to its essence and you come to the conversion of individual people. To evangelize must mean giving each man, woman and child an opportunity to hear and understand the gospel. Then, if there be response, surely there should be obedience to Matthew 28:19–20: ". . . make disciples of all the nations, baptizing them into the name of the Father and of the Son and of the Holy Ghost: teaching them to observe all things whatsoever I commanded you" (RV).

All this takes time. It means personal work like the work of our Lord Jesus by the side of the well (John 4). In India at least, souls are not saved in bunches, but one by one.

Work in the villages is not spectacular. It is hot, sometimes dull plod, with many a discouragement. But our Commander said "Go," and there is joy in obedience.

❖ At first Amy was puzzled by the difference between evangelistic work in Japan, where she saw many saved, and India. Later she understood.

In India

When first I came to India, I was astonished and grievously disappointed because I did not see what I had seen in Japan. There, before going on a special campaign, the number I might ask for and receive from Him was usually shown the day before, a day given up to prayer. And as it was shown, so it came to pass; baptism followed as a matter of course and open life as a Christian thereafter. Here it was different.

But why? Was not the power of God the same in India as in Japan? So far as I could tell, the preparation was the same. Why then were the results so different?

It seems to me now, and the missionary reading of years confirms it, that the Sovereign Master of the field sends some to parts of that field where He knows there will be tremendous strain on faith; and He trusts them to go on there and *be sure* that even there He shall reign.

It is so where individual souls are concerned. "He must reign" (1 Cor. 15:25). The word has gone forth, and the day will come when we shall hear great voices in heaven saying, "The kingdoms of this world are become the kingdoms of our Lord and of his Christ" (Rev. 11:15).

We live in the interval between Calvary and that day of

days. The Two Witnesses have a word for us. They stand in the Presence. "These are the two olive trees and the two candlesticks standing before the God of the earth" (Rev. 11:4). They have power. They have traffic with heaven "as often as they will." But the Beast that ascends out of the bottomless pit shall overcome them and kill them. No waving of palms here, no harvest fields. Defeat, death to all human hopes (Rev. 11:7).

But the end? "The Spirit of life from God entered into them. . . . And they heard a great voice from heaven saying unto them, Come up hither" (Rev. 11:11–12).

There can't be any such thing as "no result" if truly and faithfully, and in the power of the Spirit, the message is given.

❖ More and more Amy realized that all who sought the salvation of souls were engaged in a battle with invisible forces of darkness. Before they could venture forth to proclaim the gospel, there must be much prayer and careful preparation, time spent quietly waiting on the Lord to discover His plan of action.

Standing in God's Counsel

Jeremiah 23:22 is surely intensely solemn for us. "*If* they had stood in my counsel, and had caused my people to hear my words, then they should have turned them from their evil way, and from the evil of their doings."

So the measure of our power to win souls depends upon the reality of our standing in His counsel. When we live very close to Him, deep in Him, He is able to *show* us His thoughts and plans about things and people so that we can work along His lines instead of across them; and He can lead us straight to the hearts He has been preparing, and all we do will be backed by His power.

Those of us who have tried to work, and work *hard*, without having first "stood in His counsel," know how like fighting upstream it is. One's words seem to hit against a wall, or float into the air, or drop into the sea. They feel, and surely are, just purposeless waste.

Oh! Do let us ask for each other a more and more real standing in the presence of our God.

Listening

"Give Thy servant a listening heart" (1 Kings 3:9, Kay). "The secret converse of the Lord (*colloquium familiare*) is with them that fear Him" (note on Ps. 25:14, Kay).

> What do I know of listening? O my Father,
>   Teach me in silence of the soul to gather
> Those thoughts of Thine that, deep within me flowing,
>   Like currents of a river, guide my going.
>
> Light of Thy Spirit in me, fainter, clearer,
>   Burneth and shineth, as I further, nearer,
> Stand toward that light. O steady my decision
>   To wait in silence for the heavenly vision.
>
> But not for luxury of spiritual rapture
>   Would I thus wait; but as the bird doth capture
> The purposed note, so I, obedient, bringing
>   The purposed work, would offer it with singing.

A Fight of Faith

It is a fight—a fight of faith against an ever-present, powerful but invisible foe. Continually I find it needful to remind myself that an unseen foe is not less powerful because unseen. Once inadvertently I touched a live wire. The voltage was not strong enough to kill (this is a glimpse of the obvious!) but it was strong enough to strike my arm down as with the blow of a mallet. I shall never forget my startled sense of the might of an invisible force, as I stood there for a moment stricken and almost frightened, so direct, so personal the blow.

Invisible but awfully powerful is that with which we have to do when we pray for the salvation of even a baby-soul. Here, where Satan himself is openly worshiped, the power that is often exercised through witchcraft is amazing.

❖ All through her life from her earliest days, Amy expressed herself in verse, often "doggerel" made up on the spur of the moment, full of humor and fun, but often too endeavoring to put into words her deepest feelings. The following poem, sent to her first prayer supporters, is a mixture of the two:

Resignation

There are some brave souls, and God knows them well,
Though magazines may not their praises swell,
    Whose life breathes a fragrance, just felt, not seen,
    Like the scent of the violet lost in green.
      Trusted with pain in a shaded room,
      Trusted with office, or shop, or loom,
      Trusted with pen or needle or broom,
    Such, day by day, toil, suffer and pray,
    Contented to serve their God any way.
But some there are, super-finely molded,
Who sit with hands submissively folded;
    Who vegetate rather than live, and suggest

Good cabbages—doing no harm at best.
　Of the poor dark world's dark need they know;
　They take a great interest in missions, and oh!
　At times they are almost ready to go—
But then, by some flaw in their calculation,
They mistake laziness for resignation.

For they are so speedily persuaded
That all the reasons by which they are aided
　To gravitate back to the easy chair
　Are fully as solid as they are fair.
　　They "can't be spared," they have surely heard,
　　And they don't recollect the rather absurd
　　Little fad that, most certainly, never a word
　Would be raised did the question involve a *Ring*,
　For "Of course, that is quite a different thing."

They have "so few gifts," and they "cannot speak";
'Tis their "*cross* in life" to be timid and weak—
　Alas that we call by such sacred name
　Excuses, invented to save us from pain,
　Far, far removed from the Cross and shame!
　　Perhaps the Society's door was locked
　　When with somewhat uncertain knuckle they knocked,
　And everyone said, "Ah! now it is plain
　You cannot be meant to try again.
　　How terrible should you the business shirk
　　Of life's most serious fancy-work
　　For our Father's business in temple's murk!"
　They sigh, and suppose so. The argumentation
　Transforms laziness into resignation.
If such a deluded one reads this rhyme
Oh will not she waken while there is time?
　Don't think that "Sit still" must infallibly be

A life-motto written expressly for thee.
　　It may be the word is "Go forward"—if not,
　　If before the Master you stand in your lot,
　　He will flame your soul with a burning hot
And passionate fire, and you shall know
The joy of setting some other aglow.

And now, won't you face it, and have a cremation
Of the laziness which you called "resignation"?

❖   Though she longed for more to hear the call of God to the mission field, Amy only wanted those who were filled with the Holy Spirit and totally committed to the Lord's service. She wrote:

The Holy Spirit's Fullness

Perhaps this may speak to someone who is thinking of offering for India—or for anywhere. It is from the *Regions Beyond* magazine, May 1887. "It seems to me, if I had come to India at all sceptical about the truth of the doctrine of the baptism or filling of the Holy Ghost for service, all doubt would have been removed. There must needs have been made such a provision as this for the man sent to work in a field like India. The man who does not know from actual experience what it is to be filled—up to his present capacity—with the Holy Spirit, *had far better* not come to India to work."

I have been thinking much of late of those words in Romans 12:11, "*Fervent in spirit.*" The Tamil gives a word which means "heat as of fever, warmth, glow, fire." His ministers, "a flame of fire"! (Heb. 1:7). Let us ask it for each other, this divine soul-fervor, the gift of the Holy Spirit: no mere fleshly earnestness, but the Spirit's energy. "The flashes thereof are flashes of fire—a very flame of the Lord."

If any missionaries on the face of the earth need to believe in the Holy Spirit, we Indian missionaries do. Pray that we may know that Power as we do not yet, and that we will *believe to see* Him conquering.

❖   Amy always applied to herself what she wrote to others, and her letters are full of requests for prayer.

Weaving for God

Sometimes Faust's lines spin themselves into fear for me:

'Tis thus at the roaring loom of Time I ply,
And weave for God the garment thou seest Him by.

Solemn, is it not? We are weaving for God the garment, *the only garment*, they may ever see Him by. Will you ask that we may be saved from ever, by word or look or gesture, pushing a soul back into the dark? Please pray for power rightly to wield the weapon of words. "Expert in war" (Song of Sol. 3:8)— that's what we want to be. And pray for the clothing of the Spirit, without which all weapons fall pointless.

❖   One of Amy's earliest letters from Japan contained an earnest plea for prayer for missionaries, missionaries in all countries of the world. She would make the same plea today.

Prayer Telegrams

In a far-away land a sister of yours wakens one morning feeling "blue." Perhaps she has been to a late meeting the night before and is tired, and the devil has a rather mean way of teasing tired people. Perhaps she has got discouraged; perhaps she is very homesick. Suddenly a sweet love-note is flashed to her from the Lord who knows our frame—a scrap of psalm or hymn, a promise long known. His felt presence, a nearness never known in less lonely days, soothes and thrills her; and the consciousness comes, "Someone is praying for me."

Or perhaps she is trying to give the message, in very visible weakness, in much fear and trembling, knowing it may be that someone is listening for the first and last time, hardly knowing what to say, hardly daring to say anything for fear of saying the wrong thing. Then comes a prayer telegram, and in the power of the Holy Spirit, the word is spoken fearlessly. As distinctly as if a voice had told her so, she knows it is the answer to a home prayer rising then.

Temptations and testings come, insidious little things, scarcely recognizable at first, "subtle wiles" indeed. The climate tries her. She misses home friends and home ways. Trifles have a power to fret and chafe. Perhaps study or service press in and hinder quiet with Him who says, "Be still and know" (Ps. 46:10). It is terribly possible to get out of touch. She feels it, and shrinks in pain and shame from the very thought. Then she learns the value of home prayers as never before, knows with a quite curious certainty that even now, in the moment of need, one of the Lord's remembrancers is reminding Him of her; knows too that He Himself has prayed for her that her faith fail not. And such reassurance comes, such rest!

Will you not send us ever so many prayer telegrams? Pray for us whenever you think of us and know that not one prayer ever miscarries, nor will the answer come too late.

❖ As in Japan, there were converts in India also, not in large numbers but individuals. Often just one from a village or caste braved the fury of family and friends and came to the mission house for shelter. It was impossible in those days for a convert to stay at home; to become a Christian meant quite literally forsaking all to follow Christ. Whenever a man, woman or child turned to Christ, the whole village closed. Instead of friendliness or at least toleration, there was bitter anger and opposition and grief. No one would receive the Lord's messengers; no one would listen to the message.

A prayer Amy wrote was set to music and is still often sung at prayer meetings:

For New Believers

O Lord, we bring Thee these for whom we pray—
    Be Thou their strength, their courage and their stay;
And should their faith flag as they run the race,
    Show them again the vision of Thy Face.

Be Thou their vision, Lord of Calvary,
    Hold them to follow, hold them fast by Thee.
O Thou who art more near to us than air,
    Let them not miss Thee ever, anywhere.

Revised in Wings, 104

Basket

2

Service

❖ On March 6, 1901, something happened which changed forever Amy's life and work. The story is best told in her own words in *Gold Cord*, published in 1932. Briefly, a seven-year-old girl escaped from a temple house and fled to Amy for refuge. She was destined to be "married to the god" in the Hindu temple, which meant a life of prostitution and deified sin. Amy was pierced to the heart as she learned of this evil traffic in the souls and bodies of innocent children, and God laid on her the burden to save them, make a truly Christian home for them and train them to be witnesses to their own people.

This meant that the itinerant evangelistic work had to cease, for babies "tie the mother's feet," as the Tamil proverb puts it. For the next forty-six years (until 1947 when, after Independence, Indian reformers made the practice of dedicating little girls to the temple illegal) Amy and those who joined her devoted their whole lives to this new task.

Amy the wanderer wandered no more. She never returned to England, and she seldom left Dohnavur, the place to which God had led her by such a circuitous route.

By 1947 there were more than 900 in the family which began in 1901 with just one small child, and the Dohnavur

Fellowship had been born. Though now smaller in size, it continues to this day to save and bring up those who would otherwise be exploited or left to die.

Amy, or *Amma* (the Tamil word for "mother") as she was now called, did not plan the Dohnavur Fellowship. She had no deliberate intention of founding a community. She wrote, "We have a God who thinks beforehand for His children; we have only to follow His thoughts."

It was as she followed God's thoughts that she was led on step by step, often through painful and frightening experiences, into a new and altogether different kind of service for her Lord.

The Cloud

I thought the way upon the mountain side
Would lead to certain clearness; but my Guide,
Whose thought was otherwise,
Led to a cloud that blotted out the skies.

I feared to enter into that great cloud,
And fearing, cried aloud,
"O patient Guide, I fear;
Be not far from me now, with trouble near."

"Let not thy heart be troubled. Could I cease
    To care for thee?
Can vapors cancel peace, My gift of peace?
    O rest in Me.
I wait to meet thee in that cloudy place,
And in that cloud thou shalt behold My face."

Small Beginnings

We were led from very small beginnings. Each move forward was a step out of the boat of safety upon the turbulent water, and we could not take that step until we were sure.

It has always been, "'Lord, if it is You, command me to come to You on the water.' So he said, 'Come'" (Matt. 14:28–29, NKJV). For every new departure there must be the word of direction, that word which is light upon the path; and there must be faith of the vital sort, faith which fears not but obeys.

❖   Amma's first need was for helpers, for the family soon became too large for her to care for with only the valiant help of the Christian women in her band. She did then what she continued to do throughout her long life: took her Bible and prayed.

Helpers

In the days when hardly anyone cared whether the children perished or not, I used to open my Bible and read aloud as a child would to one who is very near and listening, "There went with him a band of men, whose hearts God had touched" (1 Sam. 10:26). And I used to say to our God very longingly, "Where are they, Lord, those hearts that You have touched? You know that I cannot go to look for them. Look for them for me, O Lord, my God, Father of these little ones, great Toucher of hearts."

How the ancient stories live! "There separated themselves unto David men of might, and men fit for the battle. . . . Then David received them and made them captains of the band." 1 Chronicles 12:8–18 tells how it was and is.

❖   Throughout the years Amma wrote a great many letters to those who were considering joining her. Always she put before them the need to be absolutely certain of God's will.

The Call

We pray for the call, the thrusting forth. Should any read this who are at the parting of the ways, I want to say very earnestly, *Be sure of your call.* Our Lord deals variously with souls, but the soul must be sure that He and He alone is the Chooser of its path.

Do not feel the call of God is always as it were audible. It is more the quiet sense of peace that comes when one is on one's knees before Him and as one goes about one's daily work; peace, but also outward attack. Has anyone come to us unattacked? I do not know of any. Certainly all who are to bear the burden of leadership know it.

"I am not here because of choice"—to be able to say that, unshaken by all that will happen after the field is reached and the pressure of life comes on, is rest of heart. Anything less is torture.

A call is a quiet, steady pressure upon the spirit from which there is no escape. It is an assurance, a conviction.

Then there is the leading of God at the other end. If both coincide and the way is opened, let the soul go on in peace. If it be otherwise, then "The meek will he guide in judgment: and the meek will he teach his way" (Ps. 25:9). There is something else in His mind for that life, something better. He will not waste its offer of love if only it is willing that He should choose how it is to be outpoured.

❖ Amma never glossed over the cost. She was looking for fellow-workers with her own total commitment to do and be *anything* for love of the Lord and of the souls for whom He died.

The Price

There will be the price to pay. "They will not be crucified. There is too much of the natural," so someone imagined the Father saying to the Son with regard to the powerlessness of witness in the earth. He sought for messengers "crucified to the natural man and his feelings," but where were they? Where are they? Do the angels marvel that there are so few? And yet we say that we follow Him.

> He was a gambler too, my Christ;
> He took His life and threw
> It for a world redeemed.
> And ere His agony was done,
> Before the westering sun went down,
> Crowning that day with its crimson crown,
> He knew that He had won.

❖ As her children grew up, Amma needed more helpers to educate them and to train them to be witnesses to their own people. Longingly but very honestly, she wrote:

Steel

We need one, an evangelist through and through, for the preparing and leading out of those who should soon be going to their people with the word of life.

Not a word of attraction can I write to such a one. It will be desperately hard work; iron would snap under the strain of it. I ask for steel, that quality which is at the back of all going on, patience which cannot be tired out and love that loves in very deed unto death.

If anyone expects gratitude he will be disappointed. We are not here to receive gratitude but to do the will of our Father. But very often, far beyond our deserving, we find response and love.

❖ Amma did not only write letters, she also received them from all over the world. In her own writings she did not only think of her own family and her own work; she shared with others what the Lord had taught her and rejoiced in her fellowship with other members of the Lord's body, the church, wherever they might be.

The Household of God

Are we not part of what He calls His body? And He is the Head of the body, the church (Col. 1:18), the called-out ones, as the Greek word means. Where two or three, or two or three hundred, or two or three thousand, are gathered together in His name there is He in the midst of them (Matt. 18:20). His presence makes such a gathering vital. Vital union with Him makes me one of His church. So, thank God, we are part of the household of God, part of the whole family in heaven and earth (Eph. 2:19).

God's Purpose

For what purpose has God chosen us? Ephesians 1:6 and 3:10–11 give the answer to that question. We have been created to the praise of the glory of His grace—to the intent that the manifold wisdom of God might be made known by the Church to the principalities and powers in the heavenly places.

Think of the amazing wonder of those mighty beings looking on as we live our sometimes dusty lives, and think of them seeing some new beauty of their Lord in us, "wisdom that is never at a loss to carry out its purposes of grace, be the problems presented by its subject what they may."

It is a thought far beyond our understanding, but it is written, so it must be true. Today you and I, and all of us together, may by the grace of our Lord Jesus show something of our God to these heavenly beings whom we do not see now, but shall one day see.

What shall we show today? Love under provocation to unlove? Peace under stress and strain? Gentleness? Patience? Hope? Joy? Something that would never be if we were left to ourselves?

This then, the showing forth of His beauty (and "how great is his goodness, and how great is his beauty!"—Zech. 9:17) is His eternal purpose which He purposed in Christ Jesus our Lord, "in whom we have boldness and access with confidence through faith in Him" (Eph. 3:12, NKJV). Thank God for those great words.

❖ Specially dear to Amma's heart were letters from her own children. At a time when "on the dot" was the "in" word among her boys, she enjoyed a verse sent to her by one of them. "Whatsoever he says to you, do it (on the •)." Her letters often referred to this need for instant obedience and sheer hard work.

Toil

"Toil" is the word for most of the work that comes to be done. There is no flying over our Everest; we must climb it step by step, and to climb can be toilsome. I find great comfort in Way's translation of Psalm 95:4, "The mountains' toilsome heights are His." We are called to be "happy mountaineers" by One who does not underrate the toil. When it is hardest He will be nearest. We shall see Him who is invisible on the mountains, feel the grasp of His hand, hear His heartening voice. We shall "Toil unto weariness" and yet not be weary; we shall climb and not faint.

Sometimes I used to feel, "It is almost too much." Often after a broken night (nursing sick babies) someone would come with a tale of woe before six o'clock in the morning. Often there was hardly a minute's breathing space through the whole day. You all know such days; they aren't easy. They can be overwhelming.

But the curse of the fig tree was just that it would not be able to help anyone any more: "Let no one eat fruit from you ever again" (Mark 11:14, NKJV). And immediately the fig tree withered away. So the greatest possible curse is to be deprived of the power to give to others, to help others, to live for others. God grant that such a fate shall never be yours or mine.

Stick to Your Work

"I am doing a great work, so that I cannot come down: why should the work cease, whilst I leave it, and come down to you?" (Neh. 6:3). *Our* work is great because commanded by a great Master and for a great end.

When our Lord sent the Seventy forth He said, "Greet no one along the road" (Luke 10:4, NKJV). "The salutations usual among the Jews took up much time. But they had so much work to do in so short a space that they had not a moment to spare" (Wesley). Also He said, "Do not go from house to house," as if to say, "Stick to your work."

Beginnings are happy things, but it is the steady going on that counts, when the excitement has subsided and there is no very evident mounting up with wings as eagles or running without weariness. The call then is to sheer faithfulness. That is the time to count on the sustaining grace of God who enables His followers to walk and not faint.

Interruptions

Sometimes I think one's life is made up of interruptions, and then I remember Manning's words: "There never was anyone whose life was fuller of endless employment, or more broken by constant interruptions, than the life of our blessed Lord." "It is enough"—yes, and all joy and honor—"for the servant that he be as his Master" (Matt. 10:25).

But pray for us, that the work may never draw us down, or come between us and the Master. There is great danger of that where the harvest is so great and the laborers so few.

❖   Once someone wrote and asked Amma, "What is required in a leader?" She replied:

Leadership

Apart from love—which must always be—patience, a fixed purpose and grit are required in anyone who has to do with the spiritual training of younger souls, or to whom younger ones look for an example.

What is grit? That in us which sets the firmer the harder things are. Grit is the reinforced concrete of character. "It is required in stewards [leaders] that one be found faithful" (1 Cor. 4:2, NKJV). Grit is the root of faithfulness.

There is an awful loneliness in leadership. There are times when the one who is responsible for another soul can only stand alone and "look from the top"—look at the clouds of earth as one who stands above them and is not dominated by them. If I am under a cloud, under the weather, how can I help another into the sunlight of God?

In life what matters is not what happens to us but how we meet what happens. There is nothing eternal in troubles of any sort. The note of eternity sounds through one thing only—our attitude towards the events which God allows to come into our lives.

No Greater Joy

When we begin to work for God often there is an unconscious touch of selfishness in our service. There is a good deal of the "I" even in our prayers. But later something deeper comes. It was not an immature apostle who wrote, "I have no greater joy than to hear that my children walk in truth" (3 John 4).

I believe there is no greater joy than that. Even the joy of being used oneself to lead a soul to Christ pales before the joy of seeing one's spiritual children used.

The Hidden Life

When Isaiah saw the vision of the Lord sitting upon a throne high and lifted up, he saw the seraphim. But did he see their faces? "Each one had six wings; with two he covered his face" (Isa. 6:1–2, NKJV).

> Not I, but Christ, be honored, loved, exalted,
> Not I, but Christ, be seen, be known, be heard.

That is our heart's desire if indeed we have ever seen Him, ever crowned Him king. But how often we have found "this cruel self" alive and stirring within us! We have not been like the seraphim.

I wonder if there is any limit to the music that would pour through us for the uplifting and the comfort of others if only we could be trusted to live the hidden life with Christ in God, the life the winged seraphim show us?

❖ Amma was not only concerned for leaders. All service for the Lord was equally important in her eyes. She endeared herself to hundreds of ordinary people, servants, craftsmen, laborers, gardeners, all with whom she had any contact, by her genuine and unfailing gratitude for any small thing they did. Of her own family she wrote:

Hidden Service

Is enough made of the contribution the workers in the office make to the well-being of the whole community? Or the housekeepers? Or those who see to the making and mending? Or the buyers of stores in many scattered markets? Or the one who fills gaps of all sorts and never says anything about it? Or the brains that think out plans for the help of everybody, or see to something so necessary to the good of all that it is apt to be taken for granted?

Well, the Lord of the hidden servants "makes much" of each single one of these who are perhaps the least noticed in a community.

❖   Our Savior's words in John 14:12 must, she thought, "have been spoken surely with great happiness":

Greater Works

"Greater works than these shall he do; because I go unto my father" (John 14:12). I never saw the strong assurance that lies in these words as I do now, the comfort and encouragement to faith. For the one who is to do the work is not some famous person, but just a humble believer in his Captain and his Captain's ways, and a loyal follower. As a man traveling in a far country, so is our Lord. In a sense which is very real, we serve an absent Master for He has gone to His Father—He whom having not seen, we love (1 Pet. 1:8).

But in an equally real sense He is *not* in a far country, He is not absent, He is here—"Lo, I am with you always." And it is His delight so to work through the least of us that He will be able to do "greater works" than He could do if He were with us in the flesh, confined in form and place and time.

Only we must be like soldiers whose hearts are set on loyalty, that glorious loyalty that cares for nothing in all the world but pleasing Him who has chosen us to be His soldiers (2 Tim. 2:4).

❖   Many friends sent Amma books and she used to underline and share with others the thoughts she gleaned from them. One of the poems she loved links the story of Gideon in Judges 7:15–21 with 2 Corinthians 4:7, "But we have this treasure in earthen vessels, that the excellency of the power may be of God, and not of us":

Ready to Break

"Pitchers for the lamps of God!"
    Hark the cry goes forth abroad.
Not the beauty of the make
But ah! the readiness to break
    Marks the vessels of the Lord,
Meet to bear His lighted word!

That's what we want to be: *ready to break*. Just nothing in ourselves and in our thought of ourselves, that the excellency of the power may be of God and not of us.

❖ The same verse, and the same thought of the earthen vessels, inspired her own poem:

Fragrance

They say that once a piece of common clay
Such fragrance breathed as from a garden blows,
"My secret is but this," they heard it say,
"I have been near a rose."

And there are those who bear about with them
The power, with thoughts of Christ, men's hearts to stir;
For, having knelt to kiss His garment's hem,
Their garments smell of myrrh.

So grant I pray Thee, Lord, that by Thy grace
The fragrance of Thy life may dwell in me,
That as I move about from place to place
Men's thoughts may turn to Thee.

❖   Many people thought, incorrectly, that Amma was op-
posed to marriage, considering a single worker of more value
than a married one. This was not the case; instead, she herself
found much enjoyment in helping forward the marriage of
workers who fell in love. At the same time there was always
need for those who could work full time with the children,
without any home ties. As always she based her opinions on
Scripture, and although she did not quote the first part of the
following verse, she undoubtedly had it in mind:

Marriage

"I wish that all men were even as I myself. But each one has
his own gift from God, one in this manner and another in that"
(1 Cor. 7:7, NKJV). God makes it clear that two gifts are mentioned, one for the unmarried life, the other for the married.
Each equally needs the gift of the grace of God. There is no
higher and no lower. "There is no less need for a gift of grace to
use marriage Christianly, than to live Christianly otherwise."

We need the help of understanding prayer for those who
for Christ's sake and the children's have given themselves to
serve "without distraction," which, I find, means literally "without dragging in different directions." This work could not possibly be done if no one gave herself or himself to that undistracted
life. For all such the word is always,

> If Thy dear Home be fuller, Lord,
>   For that a little emptier
> My house on earth, what rich reward
>   That guerdon were.

To say this and go on saying it from the heart, and living it
in peacefulness, requires a continual inflow of heavenly enrich-
ments.

❖ Service in India, or indeed anywhere on earth, was not Amma's only aim. Constantly her thoughts and hopes and imagination were fixed on the glorious prospect of her Lord's return in glory. She longed that she herself, and all others, should be ready for that Day.

The Lord's Return

We are chosen to be those on whom the Lord can count for any manner of service when He returns. When our Lord returns to earth again, this time to deliver His people, we are told that He brings a company with Him (Zech. 14:5). This company is composed of members of the invisible church.

In the parable of the pounds (Luke 19:11–27) we are shown the faithful servant having authority over cities. To have authority means to serve to the uttermost, with no thought of self. Such service calls for disciplined spirits. "If we endure, we shall also reign with him" (2 Tim. 2:12). The first two servants rose to the call, the third failed.

This parable seems to show how the prepared, disciplined servants of the Lord will be used after the Lord has returned. There is a definite service of some sort prepared for them, and for this they must be prepared. The only time for preparation is during the interval before the Lord returns—that is, now, today, this hour, this minute.

The Dohnavur Fellowship

❖ As the family grew, it became legally necessary to form an association which could own land and property; and so the Dohnavur Fellowship was officially registered in 1927. It was in many ways an expression of what Amma was and what she had learned from God over the years.

It is impossible to understand her writings without first grasping the fact that she was utterly devoted to the work she knew God had given her. Towards the end of her life she found a new thought in an unlikely place (she was good at doing that!). "For thus says the Lord: You are Gilead to me" (Jer. 22:6).

"That's it!" she exclaimed excitedly. "That's what I am. *I am Dohnavur*—all that I am, lost in the beloved place."

If she was Dohnavur, what is the Dohnavur Fellowship? Its object is stated as follows in its "Memorandum of Association":

To save children in moral danger; to train them to serve others; to succor the desolate and the suffering; to do anything that may be shown to be the will of our heavenly Father, in order to make His love known, especially to the people of India.

The pattern for the fellowship evolved gradually. Amma wrote:

Our Special Call

For us the special call is to serve our generation by doing ordinary things to the glory of God. It is not scriptural to divide life into sections and call one secular, the other sacred. *All is sacred.* Our Lord's walk on earth shows no other attitude of mind. He recognized no dividing line. So why should we?

The one aim of all our work is to lead each man, woman and child to our Savior and to teach them how to follow Him as dear children (Eph. 5:1), and thus to prepare them for His use and lead them out into His service.

The ideal shown us is, as regards each other, loyalty, love and vital unity; and towards our Lord loving obedience, the joy of faith and lowly adoration.

Basket

3

The Bible and First Principles

❖ No one can read Amma's writings without realizing that she was steeped in the thoughts and words of the Scriptures. She read avidly every new translation and every scholarly commentary which came her way, but she died before the modern versions she would have loved so much were published. The King James Bible, or Authorized Version, was her very life.

Her teaching about the truth of the Bible was clear and uncompromising. To her growing-up children she wrote:

The Truth of the Bible

My point of view is determined by where I stand. A mountain is too great a thing for one man to see it whole. Ten men may be equally near to it and yet each has a different view of it, because his point of view is different.

So with the great mountain of Truth. No man can see truth as a whole. Truth is far too great for that. We must wait for heavenly vision before we can see as God sees, not in part because of our point of view, but in whole.

Perhaps that is something which will not come immediately even in heaven. It may mean an eternity of learning to apprehend that marvelous mountain, not from our point of view but from God's, which includes all. So let us not judge another for seeing a view that is not ours. Let us meet on the one thing that matters. We both see the mountain and rejoice in its glory. And, happy thought, we both meet on the summit.

In practice this means that we all agree in believing whatever our Lord meant by whatever He said; it does not mean that we must all hold the same interpretation of His word.

The Bible Speaks

Believing in the truth of the Bible doesn't imply that we find every part of the Book equally precious. The whole is a jewel box. There are differences in the jewels. For example, the Gospel of John is much more to us than some portions of the Old Testament, but God has a reason for every page. We mustn't say, "That could have been omitted without loss." Nothing could have been omitted without loss; if it could have been, it would not be in the Bible.

Never try to prove something by quoting an isolated text. See 1 Corinthians 2:13 comparing "spiritual things with spiritual," for guidance about that. Stand on the Rock and look at the ocean, not a single pool. Psalm 25:17 in Cheyne's translation is, "Enlarge the straitness of my heart."

In our spiritual youth we are helped by archaeological and other like arguments, but as we go on we want something deeper. The archaeological, historical, geographical accuracies are, as it were, steps leading to higher proofs which are spiritual. Energized by the Spirit of God, the words of the Scriptures speak directly to our hearts. The Bible finds us where we are. It speaks to our conditions. We all know what it is when a word seems to take life and leap from the page. It is as if we had never read it before. It throbs with spirit and life.

❖ Amma's own writings show how often this was true for her. It was true for her children too, and she tells of an incident with a young *accal* (Indian sister) who had given her life to bring up children for love of her Lord. The word that seemed to "take life and leap from the page" came in an unexpected and often neglected part of the Bible, as Amma's note shows:

The Spirit's Sword

A very precious *accal*, whose life blesses a group of children, had become disheartened. Her senior *accal* had, she thought, not understood her. Such difficulties occur everywhere, where older ones find it hard to realize that younger ones grow up.

This particular *accal*, who is really a very capable young woman, had made up her mind to come to me and ask to be changed to some other part of the work. While in this state of mind she began to read her Bible as usual, not in the least expecting what she found in Ecclesiastes: "If the spirit of the ruler rises against you, do not leave your post; for conciliation pacifies great offenses" (10:4, NKJV). *Do not leave your post*: that settled the matter. As she told me about it and read the [Tamil] verse, she lifted the Bible in her two hands and kissed it.

Isn't that Book amazing? It is always astonishing us by giving us the very word we need, the word that is life to us. This is to me the greatest proof of the divine origin of the Scriptures. The sword has an edge. It does what it says it will do. It cuts. And at the same time it heals—that is the marvel of it.

When I said, "But the spirit of the ruler didn't really rise against you; *accal* only meant to help you," the dear girl smiled and her eyes were full of love for her *accal*.

"Yes, I know that now," she said, "and yet, had it truly been as I then thought it was, the word to me was *Do not leave your post.*"

Discernment in Reading

In reading Paul's letters to the churches, we should distinguish between what was meant for a particular community at a particular time and what is for all communities and for all time. When we read either the Old or New Testament, we should read thoughtfully and spiritually, not slavishly. Our Lord taught us that, and Paul emphasizes it when he says, "The letter kills, but the Spirit gives life" (2 Cor. 3:6, NKJV).

John Wycliffe's rule is excellent: "It shall greatly helpe ye to understande Scripture, if thou mark not only what is spoken or wrytten but of whom and to whom with what words at what time, where, to what intent, with what circumstances, considering what goeth before and what followeth."

As to difficulties, "Never let what you know be disturbed by what you do not know" was the wise word of a Bible teacher long ago. As we go on in life, many difficulties disappear; life explains them. Others remain to be answered afterwards.

In this connection Deuteronomy 29:29 is a great word: "The secret things belong unto the Lord our God: but those things which are revealed belong unto us and to our children for ever, that we may do all the words of this law."

Feed Your Faith

My oldest warrior friend, Mary Hatch, writing to me lately says something which I believe will help many. "Years ago I saw a sentence in an American paper which has stuck to me: 'A Christian may feed his doubts, feed his uncertainties until all about him will be cloudy and dark; *but if he will feed his faith he will win.*'"

She says that hundreds of times on dark days she has reinforced her faith by repeating these words to herself. Our Bible is full of the essence of such words. "You will keep him in perfect peace whose mind [imagination] is stayed on You, because he trusts in You" (Isaiah 26:3, NKJV) is one of the sheer anchors of the soul in rough weather.

The General Tenor of Scripture

Once when I was in the Forest looking after some building work, I was held up by the words in Galatians 6:8: "For he who sows to his flesh will of the flesh reap corruption, but he who sows to the Spirit will of the Spirit reap everlasting life" (NKJV). Was *this* sowing to the Spirit? All day long carpenters, masons, coolies had to be seen to. There were endless small trifles to deal with. It all seemed wholly mundane, not spiritual at all. It did not look like sowing to the Spirit.

But as I read on I came to verse 10, "As we have opportunity, let us do good to all, especially to those who are of the household of faith." Those for whom I was doing this belonged to the household of faith. The work was for their good.

That settled everything, not for then only but for always. The day was filled with peace for me.

In this case the second word which balanced the first lay

alongside. Sometimes it doesn't. So we need to read largely to get the general trend, the tenor of Scripture. A good prayer for times of doubt is Psalm 119:133, "Direct my steps by Your word" (NKJV).

Teaching the Bible

In teaching Scripture, do earnestly seek to be vital. Never quote a text carelessly. Never take a Bible class carelessly. Soak yourself beforehand in the passage you are going to teach. Point by point, if you are in earnest about this, you will find it comes alive.

There is nothing as deadly as a dull Bible class, except perhaps a "dull address." I have heard it said, "He gave an address on such and such a subject." The Lord save you from giving addresses. Give a message or don't speak at all. A message means that you have listened and received something to give. Your ear has heard; your mouth must speak. There is fire and force in a living message from the living God. It is a deadly thing to give one's own words. They are sawdust. "What is the chaff to the wheat?" says the Lord (Jer. 23:28, NKJV).

Love, and your words will burn and glow. You will speak as one on whose lips a live coal from off the altar has been laid afresh before each new Bible class. God grant that it may be so.

Reverence

"Then he said, 'Do not draw near this place. Take your sandals off your feet, for the place where you stand is holy ground'" (Exod. 3:5, NKJV).

While thinking of this word this morning I found something new to me. Those who have *Young's Analytical Concordance* will find it there. Many of the most familiar verses, which we constantly quote, contain the word which may be translated "reverence."

The secret of the Lord is with them that *reverence* Him. His eye is upon them to deliver their soul from death. The angel of the Lord encamps around them. The Lord pities them, and His mercy is upon them. He gives meat to them; He fulfills their desire; He takes pleasure in them. It is for them that the Sun of Righteousness arises with healing in His wings (Ps. 25:14, 33:18, 34:7, 103:13, 111:5, 145:19, 147:11; Mal. 4:2).

These are a few of the places where this word is used by the Spirit. Rotherham translates it "revere." "The intimacy of the Lord is with them that revere him" is his beautiful rendering of Psalm 25:14.

May the Lord give us more of this reverence inwardly, and so of course outwardly too. We need reverence in our speaking to Him—see Abraham's feeling about that in Genesis 18:27, "Indeed now, I who am but dust and ashes have taken it upon myself to speak to the Lord" (NKJV)—in our speaking of Him, and in our whole life.

There will be a great overflowing of gladness in such a life. The delightfulness of meeting one another, for example, will not be less but more. "They who revere Thee shall see me and rejoice" (Ps. 119:74, Rotherham) is an enchanting word. We can turn it into, "I who revere You will see them and rejoice"— what a word for happy mealtimes!

But it will be a hallowed joy, like a feast in view of the Burning Bush, our shoes still off.

Reading Aloud

Once when we were staying in the Church Missionary Society house in Madras, Mr. Langdale-Smith took family prayers. He read Psalm 57 in such a way that I can never forget it. Thousands of times, I suppose, the words, "My heart is fixed, O God, my heart is fixed; I will sing, and give praise" (v. 7) have come back to me and strengthened my heart.

God can use the way you read His words aloud to do eternal work. Don't think it waste of time to pray over what you are going to read to others. Our God can so kindle your own heart, and put such a tone into your voice, that those words will live forever in the hearts of those who listen.

❖ Amma's teaching was always based on her own experience and practice. She did not depend on her own outstanding gifts as a speaker, but on the Holy Spirit. Every year on her birthday, there was a special meeting for her family in which she put before them the way of salvation and the claims of Christ on their lives as individuals. There was much prayer-preparation both before and after the meeting. She wrote:

The Birthday Meeting

Pray for the kindling of the Holy Spirit. I do so dread any fleshly energy or movement. Pray that it all may be solid and real. Ask that power to lead to decision may be given—no mere stirred feeling, but action—pray for that.

Zechariah 4:6 is wonderful and more wonderful than ever in Tamil! "By strength NOT, by power NOT, by My Spirit ONLY, the God of Armies says." Don't we often try to help God, forgetting it must be only "by the Spirit of the God of Armies"?

But finally, let us *expect*. We have prayed for the binding of the powers of evil; let us expect, then. And yet (for often the deepest work is done very quietly and at first without observation) don't let us be disappointed if we don't see all we long to see, and don't let us be shocked or disappointed out of hoping for anyone.

❖ One year, when illness prevented her from giving the message herself, she gave the notes she had prepared to someone else. This was her message to her big family, translated of course into Tamil.

The Birthday Message

Every morning I hear the postman's bell. I know that in a minute or two a heap of letters will be poured out and someone will go and look through them carefully. Presently some of those letters will be brought to me, but not all. Only those will be brought that are addressed to me. I have nothing to do with the other letters. I may not open one of them. They are not to me. Only those addressed to me are for me.

It is very important to make no mistake about this. If I opened *Annachie's* [elder brother's] letter by mistake I should be very much ashamed and distressed, and if he opened mine he would feel just the same. He would not read even a postcard that was addressed to me, nor would I read even a postcard that was addressed to him.

But if a letter came that was addressed to the whole family, we should all be free to read it. If however we found a sentence written to one of us by name, *that* sentence would be special to the one for whom it was written. Though others might read it, it would really belong to the one for whom it was intended.

The Bible is like an open letter and so we may all read it, but there are many sentences in it which are meant for special people only. It is almost as if the names of those special ones were written on the page.

There are some here who did truly give themselves to the Lord Jesus once and trust Him to save them, and yet today they know they are not close to Him. They have wandered from Him and are doing things to please themselves now, and not their Lord. They are not living for their Savior. And they are miserable, and deep in their hearts they are longing to come back to Him, but they are ashamed and don't know what to say.

The words I have been given for the Birthday meeting are to them. It is just as if the name of that boy, girl, man, woman were written on the margin of the page beside Hosea 14:1.

"O . . . . . ." (here put your name) "return to the Lord your God, for you have stumbled because of your iniquity" (NKJV).

Do you feel, "I am not fit to return"? This is true, but you cannot hurt the love of God more than by staying away.

Do you feel, "I don't know what to say to Him"? He tells you what to say. Say, "Take away all iniquity" (Hosea 14:2).

All. Not "All except that dear sin, that private sin, that I want to keep a little longer." All means all. Think a minute. Do you want to let go *all*?

If you do, then this also is for you, "Receive us graciously."

Dear children, I have known our Father much longer than any of you and I have never once known Him refuse to hear that prayer. Trust His great love.

Can you imagine how much love there would be in this House of Prayer if you could put in one big heap all the love of my heart for you all, and all your *Sitties'* [mother's younger sister] and *Annachies'* [elder brother] and *Accals'* [elder sister] love, and all the love of the people in England and Germany and Switzerland and France and Sweden and Australia and New Zealand and America and Canada who pray for you and send us money to buy all we need? Can you imagine that big heap of love? It would reach higher than the visitors' gallery, it would reach up to the roof and beyond the roof, I think.

But the love of God reaches up above that, far, far above that. Look up into the blue sky by day, or into the starry sky at night, and think, "God's love fills all that space."

No words can describe its length and depth and breadth and height for it passes knowledge. It is *this* love that longs over you when you sin and fall. It is *this* love that calls you now. Return. Return.

What next?

And then, what next? A friend of mine once gave me a box full of little drawers. In each drawer were stones of different kinds. I gave this box to Nesa Sittie and it is in the *Jeevalia* [Girls' School] now. Since then, several times I have wanted stones out of that box, but not one stone was in my room. When I gave the box to Nesa Sittie, I gave her all the drawers and that meant all the stones in the drawers.

The box was mine to give. I gave it. It is not mine now, nothing in its little drawers belongs to me.

It was like that with a calf a Jew brought to the priest as a sacrifice to God. Once he gave it he could not take part of it back. It was all given. So when we read the words, "We will offer the sacrifices of our lips" (Hos. 14:2, NKJV) we know the meaning is, "I give You my lips as a gift, a sacrifice. I will not take my lips back and use them for myself. They shall not belong to me any more."

And just as all the stones in all the drawers of the box were included in the gift of the box, so all the words my lips say are included in the gift of my lips. They are not mine now. I have no right at all to speak words for my own pleasure only, or untrue or unkind or silly words. True, kind, happy words, words pleasing to my Lord, are the only words I have any right to speak with lips that are really given up to Him.

Is it not true that nearly always *words* (untrue, unkind, silly) have a great deal to do with our falls? The only safe way then is to give up our lips altogether. Many ask God to save their souls and take them to heaven, and they stop there; but God does not stop there. He wants the *lips* of Christians, not only their souls. "Present your bodies a living sacrifice"(Rom. 12:1).

Beautiful promises follow in Hosea. God will be dew to us, rain to us. He will make us grow as the lily and be strong as the trees on our mountains. But that this may be, come to Him. Come for the first time if you have not come before. Return to Him if you have been wandering. Yield all—soul, lips, *all*.

O by His eternal love I beseech you, do not refuse His call today. He is waiting to hear your answer. What will it be?

PRINCIPLES

❖   Amma was not only the mother of a very large family, she was also the leader of a close-knit community. She did not make "rules" for the community—all the rules needed were to be found in the Bible—but she did sometimes write down for them the principles she considered essential. First and foremost, and indeed all-inclusive, was love.

Keep the Law of Love

Don't make it harder for your fellows to be good. If wrong is in question, carefully observe our Lord's command: "If you bring your gift to the altar, and there remember that your brother has something against you, leave your gift there before the altar, and go your way. First be reconciled to your brother, and then come and offer your gift" (MATT. 5:23–24, NKJV). Remember too our Lord's teaching in Matthew 18:15–17. Unless the wrong-doer is ill in mind or body and unable for a direct word, never speak about him to another till you have first gone to him or her.

But before speaking, make sure there is wrong to put right. Don't be critical. Don't be suspicious. If you possibly can, believe the best and kindest was meant.

Be tender. You don't know the stress under which the one perhaps was, when the troubling word was spoken. Don't be hard on anyone.

Romans 12:9 (RV), "Let love be without hypocrisy," yes; but also Ephesians 4:15, "speaking the truth in love." Drench the words in love before you speak them, considering yourself and how often *you* need forgiveness.

Never take offense; that is petty. Never criticize. We should feel safe with one another.

If you are ever hurried into writing a hot letter, keep it over night to cool. You know the old illustration: Fill a glass with sweet milk. Does a rough jolt make it spill out something sour? May the Lord of all sweetness fill our hearts with sweetness.

Unless our letters burn with a living love to the living Lord and in some way show Him for what He is—*Love on fire*—what are they? Ashes. God save us from scattering ashes.

Never, never let a root of bitterness spring up. It is a most dangerous and defiling thing. If you water that root with un-kind thoughts it will bring forth poisonous fruit. Love—"Be-loved, let us love. For all the law is fulfilled in one word, even in this: *'You shall love'*" (1 John 4:7; Gal. 5:14, NKJV).

❖ The only source of guidance and strength for the fellow-ship was through prayer, and for that to be effective there had to be vital unity. This unity was (and is) always under attack, and Amma wrote many notes to warn and counsel her fel-low-workers. Some she called:

A Few Don'ts

Don't strain out gnats. Some call the Bible the "Word" and spell it with a capital letter. Some don't because of John 1:1 (and compare Hebrews 4:12). Don't quibble over such things. Those who speak and write so, do it in reverence.

Some call Sunday the Lord's Day, others call it First Day. Both are scriptural, but there is no need to get into bondage over the matter.

Some keep special days; some esteem every day alike. Paul did not seem to think this a matter of importance. Some are uncomfortable if they see a cross anywhere; others see in the empty cross the sign of what they do most earnestly believe and wish to hold in their hearts.

Some feel read prayers are not prayers at all, forgetting that hymns and sacred songs are prayers. Don't argue such points. Leave them, remembering that no prayer, read or otherwise, is prayer at all unless the soul is on her knees.

There are dozens of such little superficial things that might be named, but it is not worthwhile to rake them up. The great thing to remember is, don't worry over words like a dog over a bone. Don't be one with whom others have to be careful. It is very restful in friendship to be able to walk into one another's room (the mind is a room) without fear of upsetting the furniture.

Unity

An illustration of the powerlessness of opposite views to separate fellow-lovers is found in Peter and Paul's home life. Peter had a wife. Paul hadn't. To Paul's way of thinking, to serve the Lord without distraction meant something different from what it meant to Peter—for surely we may take it for granted that Peter also served with his whole heart. But this difference in views never came between them. To Peter, Paul was "beloved brother," and from his letters we know what Peter meant by "beloved."

There is no promise that we shall see eye-to-eye here and now. We shall see eye-to-eye when the Lord returns (Isa. 52:8, RV). But the deeper our love for one another, the more we shall be conscious of our oneness and the less we shall be conscious of differences.

No Divisions

Sometimes there is no question of different points of view. One way is eternally right, the other way eternally wrong. See 1 Corinthians 1:10–13. Dr. Way paraphrases verse 10 thus: "I entreat you, my brothers, by the dear name of our Lord Jesus the Messiah, to be unanimous in the profession of your faith. Let there be no divisions among you: let unity be restored in purpose and in creed." Conybeare's translation is: "I exhort you, brethren, by the name of our Lord Jesus Christ, to shun disputes, and have no divisions among you, but to be knit together in the same mind and the same judgment."

Godet writes that Paul wants "full harmony of view in regard to Christian truth, and then perfect agreement in the way of resolving particular questions," for he has heard that some claim him as leader, some Apollos, some Peter, some Christ. "Was Paul crucified for you?" he asks, as if to pierce their very hearts. The words must have burned out of him; and then, surely, those contentious people must have been melted together in bitter shame and grief.

So it seems to me that the passage deals with far deeper things than views. It touches Christian thinking, Christian living. It leaves us once more broken in the presence of the Crucified.

❖ Amma had a tremendous sense of the value of time, of every minute as a trust from God to be lived to the full for His purposes alone. This colored much of her thinking and her counseling.

The Preciousness of Time

Time is racing past us. Once past us, it is irrecoverable. "Yesterday now is part of forever"—so is the minute that we have just now lived.

We cannot flow both deep and wide. Only God can do that. We have only a limited number of days to live and only a limited quantity of energy to spend. So the important thing is to spend ourselves as entirely as possible upon whatever is our special calling—our vocation.

The World

We do care about the world at large. We care to know about it. It is right to give thought to what is going on. Our Lord did, or He could not have described it as He did. But the day has only twelve hours, and "First the Kingdom" is our watchword. "Did you not know that I must be about My Father's business?" (Luke 2:49, NKJV). We know what our Father's business for us is. Let us do it. If we do it faithfully, it will demand all our energies and occupy our whole time.

We can best help the world by prayer and by humble, faithful service; not by agitation and criticism, but by patience, prayer and love.

When the heart is overwhelmed by many thoughts concerning the state of the world, could there be anything more strengthening than the calm words written so long ago in Psalm 103:19? "The Lord has established His throne in heaven, and His kingdom rules over all" (NKJV).

However things appear, whatever turmoil may fill the world, whoever may imagine himself mighty, there is this certainty upon which we rest. Look where you will, you see problems. The only thing is to look above them all. "The Lord God Omnipotent reigns" (Rev. 19:6). Our unseen Leader has never known defeat nor ever will.

The world is God's world. The people in the world are dear to God: "God so loved the world that He gave. . . ." "All souls are mine," He says (Ezek. 18:4). "World politics" is only a short way of alluding to all that has ever happened and all that is happening in the world—the concerns of God in the world.

We need to be careful to think along His lines and in His presence. If we turn from our newspapers excited and fussed, it is clear that we have not read the news in His presence but in the presence of His enemy, whose aim is to distract us from what matters more than news. Our reaction should be a quickened sense of the preciousness of souls, and so of those souls with whom we have to do.

We are not of this world. Our citizenship and so all our chief interests are elsewhere. The fact that Christians do not generally live as if this were true makes no difference to its truth. See Romans 12:2 (NKJV) for the practical outworking of this truth: "Do not be conformed to this world, but be transformed by the renewing of your mind, that you may prove what is that good and acceptable and perfect will of God."

It follows then that, as our Lord told Pilate, we do not fight with swords to win the Kingdom. The so-called wars of religion were utterly wrong. Our Lord Jesus showed us by His example, which is the one example we are meant to follow, that spiritual victories are won not by the weapons of earth but by suffering, tears and death.

❖ Once, at their request, Amma summarized the principles on which the fellowship was founded, for the benefit of a group of Indian men who were taking increasing responsibility as leaders. They used to meet with her regularly for discussion, Bible study and prayer, and she gave them the following notes:

PRINCIPLES

Fundamental Truth as Basis of Reasoning

1 *That God is.*
Hebrews 11:6

So in all things He must have the pre-eminence. To do His will is our one supreme concern.

2 *That He is the Rewarder of them that diligently seek Him.*
Hebrew 11:6

So we may count upon His presence, His guidance and His provision. The certainty of the fulfillment of all His promises is included in this also.

3 *That to live as seeing Him who is invisible is possible.*
Hebrew 11:27

So out of weakness we can be made strong. We can be more than conquerors through Him who loved us.

4 *That "we look for a City, we seek a country, a better country," expresses the attitude of life.*
Hebrews 11:10, 14

So our citizenship is in heaven, not here. (See Phil. 3:20, RV.) Such words as Philippians 3:10 and 2 Corinthians 4:10 govern our thinking. We are only here as ambassadors for Christ, and nothing matters but to please Him.

General Laws as Guide to Action

The law of love
John 13:34: "A new commandment I give to you, that you love one another; as I have loved you, that you also love one another" (NKJV).

The Gospels are full of illustrations of that "as." One that is not often noticed is in John 17:6: "They have kept your word"—overlooking so much. Love, of course, connotes also loyalty.

The law of unity
John 17:11: "Keep them that they may be one, even as we are."

The least break in unity, even the shadow of an unkind or doubting word or thought about another, is enough to kill prayer.

The law of service
Galatians 5:13: "By love serve. For all the law is fulfilled in this: You shall love."

This utterly crosses out all thought of the praise of man. It brings us to John 13:1–5; Matthew 20:27–28, 10:24, 6:19–21, 33; Luke 9:23–24.

Choice of Less Rather Than More

"Though He was rich, yet for your sakes He became poor, that you through His poverty might become rich" (2 Cor. 8:9, NKJV).

If there had been a better way, would not the Lord have shown it? And so we in the fellowship lay a special emphasis on desire (not just willingness but *desire*) to do without things we might have, so that there may be more to give.

These are mountain-peak thoughts. Compare the groveling life of petty ambitions, petty doings, petty chatter, tittle-tattle and that horrid thing, backbiting, with the kind of life commanded by the General Law which is our "Guide to Action."

Love	*Loyalty*
Unity	*Service*

These are great words, golden words.

Arrows

"And he said to them all, If any man will come after me, let him deny himself, and take up his cross daily, and follow me" (Luke 9:23). When these words of our Lord—words neither withdrawn nor canceled—are obeyed, then the arrows of the archer fly. And so few, even of the Lord's own, stand by those who are called to this obedience that often it seems as if they, even they, were shooting those grievous arrows.

But there is a beautiful word in Judges 5:11 (RV). It opened to me one day when I could hardly bear to see someone being hurt. "Far from the noise of archers, in the places of drawing water, there shall they rehearse the righteous acts of the Lord."

History? Poetry? Yes, but more than either. There is a place of quietness far from the noise of archers, where the wounded soul draws water from the well of Living Water. "He who dwells in the secret place of the Most High shall abide under the shadow of the Almighty" (Ps. 91:1, NKJV). And he who abides there has a most wonderful and manifest power, a power won through pain, to rehearse the acts of the Lord and to magnify His name.

So fear not, you who are like Joseph when the archers shot at him and wounded him (for the archers know all the tenderest places in our souls at which to shoot). Trust the love that upheld Joseph. "But his bow abode in strength, and the arms of his hand were made strong by the hands of the Mighty One of Jacob"; and he was "a fruitful bough, a fruitful bough by a fountain; his branches run over the wall" (Gen. 49:22–24, RV).

Is it not always so? By suffering and by no lesser way is won the power to bless others. Fruit and the coolness of shadow—that is what God makes His Josephs to be. So is the pain wasted? Will it seem wasted when He shows us His hands and His feet?

❖   There were constant temptations to fear for the future of the work. Many wondered what would happen when Amma herself died. Her books, her letters, her guidance and inspiration had made and supported the fellowship; and in a sense quite different from the one she herself intended, she could say, "I am Dohnavur."

Could the work continue when she was gone? Would it still be supported by the prayers and gifts of Christians all over the world?

Amma's answer to such fears was robust.

The Future

The permanence of a work of God does not depend upon the presence of the servant but of the Master. And if it be not a work of God but of mere man or woman, why should it continue?

Basket

4

Prayer and Provision

❖ The meeting place for the Dohnavur family is the House of Prayer, built in 1927, where all the main events of the family's life are celebrated. Services, meetings, school prayers, weddings, thanksgivings, celebrations, "glory days" when one of the family goes to be with the Lord—all such occasions find the family streaming into the House of Prayer. It is truly the center of the compound.

When it was built, there were set on its highest roof not one needle, as the Tamil calls the little pointed shaft that ends a gabled roof, but two. These two needles represent prayer and service, the two essentials of the Christian life which cannot exist without each other. For Amma personally, and for the work which was her very life, prayer was not a secondary matter but the key to everything.

Prayer

It seems more and more true that infinitely more important is it *to know how to pray* than to know how to work, for unprayed-for work can do nothing for eternity. We have proved that prayer is not just a holy relief for our feelings but a force which by God's might *works*.

❖ As a young missionary in Japan, her heart was first set on learning how to pray, and she wrote in one of her private home letters:

Oh to know how to pray! Surely we are verily babes in prayer. We have not as yet gone ankle-deep in the waters He meant us to swim in. The saints of old, who could win great things from God, seem to have known an inner absorption in Him, rare with us.

What has changed? Things eternal do not change. The keys which open the treasuries are not more easily turned, the powers of evil are not less strong, souls are not less precious. What then has changed? Have we? Oh to care with a deeper caring— to pray with diviner power!

It is quiet now. Longings are finding words, taking shape. I am writing them down just as they all come, fast and thick, struggling up, leaping out—

Oh for a passionate passion for souls!
    Oh for a pity that yearns!
Oh for the love that loves unto death!
    Oh for the fire that burns!
Oh for the pure prayer-power that prevails,
    That pours itself out for the lost;
Victorious prayer in the Conqueror's name,
    Oh for a *Pentecost!*

❖ She quoted this poem in full in her book, *Gold Cord*. Her desire was fulfilled, as all who knew her would agree, but all her life she was a learner in the school of prayer. She shared the lessons the Lord taught her with her family. The first was:

Detachment

God give us all *detachment* for prayer. The word is from Weymouth's translation of Luke 14:33, "No one of you who does not detach himself from all that belongs to him can be a disciple of mine."

How little we know of this detachment. It is our shame and grief that we know so little. Would half the world be unconverted today if the followers of our Lord were detached from all that belongs to them?

Such thoughts bring us to our knees; only let us beware of asking for what we are not truly in earnest to receive. God is not mocked.

We want to know more of all this. We want to live so close to Him that He can confide in us as He could in His prophets of old. "Surely the Lord does nothing, unless He reveals His secret to His servants the prophets"(Amos 3:7, NKJV).

"He made known His *ways* to Moses, His *acts* to the children of Israel" (Ps. 103:7, NKJV). "The servant does not know what his master is doing; but I have called you *friends*" (John 15:15, NKJV). Abraham—God's friend: "Shall I hide from Abraham the thing that I do?" (Genesis 18:17).

Oh for the life of dwelling deep in the secret place, where earth's sounds fall faint and God's voice whispers His secrets! This must mean giving up a great deal more time to quiet with Him than one used to think needful. It will mean letting many other things go, one's reputation among the number—the loss of all things that I may know Him (Phil. 3:10).

Difficulties in Prayer

Have you ever, as you prayed for the improbable or the

impossible, stopped short, chilled by a whisper or perhaps a blustering assertion about the futility of it all? "What difference will it make whether you pray or not?" "What is this prayer doing? What is God doing in answer to prayer?"

We pray in the mighty name of Jesus Christ our Lord. *Can* prayer in that Name be ineffective? If it cannot, why do we not see things happen?

God give and continue to give deliverance from the paralyzing whisper, "What is the use?" God grant to us spiritual deafness. ("Who is deaf as my messenger?" Isa. 42:19.) God grant us too a new penetration in prayer, a new vitality. I think sometimes our prayers are bloodless, and nothing drains them of life-blood like a whisper of fear.

Inner Wandering

Some of our most persistent distractions in prayer are the result of some inner wandering from our Lord at other times. But our God loves simplicity. He does not want us to wrap ourselves up in a sort of mournful silence. His word is always, "Only acknowledge"; "return." I am reading Jeremiah just now and have noticed this often. You know how sometimes a child will stand silent and sulky, instead of just saying, "I'm sorry," which would end the matter at once. God doesn't want us to be like that.

So let us be simple. We have an understanding Father. He loves us very much. He isn't on the lookout for things to pounce upon, but He does ask for our all and for sincerity. He is ready to "will and do" in us. He is able to keep us from wandering.

Oh what a God! "Return to your rest, O my soul, for the Lord has dealt bountifully with you" (Ps. 116:7, NKJV).

Two Unseen Companies

There are two unseen companies: one the heavenly host, the other the satanic. Both are spoken of as "principalities and powers," and both are referred to as being "in heavenly places" (Eph. 3:10, 6:12). These two companies are, so to speak, facing one another on the great, high, unseen battlefield which is as real as this earthly battlefield. There is war between them; for the war between the angels and the dragon of which we read in Revelation 12:7 did not begin in AD 96, nor has it ended yet.

So let us lift our eyes to the invisible. We need to realize the awful might of the dark powers if we are to pray with any sort of urgency. But we need to remember the angelic host too and above all the Captain of that host whose war this is; for if we do not, we shall never pray with truly conquering faith.

We have not come to the end of that fight. This is the end: "The dragon fought and his angels *and prevailed not.*" Alleluia!

Waiting

All who pray and believe to see, *will see.* It is only a matter of waiting for a while—waiting in full confidence and joy of faith.

The children are sometimes given a kind of parched pulse of which they are very fond. The tiniest children of all find it hard to hold open their hands long enough to be filled. Very often they shut them in the middle with only a few grains inside, and the rest, falling on their little shut fingers, drops off and is lost.

It has been to me a very clear parable of the prayer that will not wait for a full answer.

❖   There was not always victory in prayer, but there was always a pressing on.

Carry Through in Prayer

There had been a call for a barrage of prayer, after what had appeared to be a victory, and it had not been given in any effective measure. *It had stopped too soon*, and in Dohnavur there was defeat.

Prayer of the kind that was needed is a labor. It is easy to accept too readily the suggestion that it is too tiring. This stopping too soon in prayer is a fatal thing.

We have a new watchword now, it is "Carry through." In Darby's translation of Ephesians there is this note on 6:13: "And having accomplished all things to stand: It may be translated 'having overcome all things,' in the same sense. It is *to carry through and put in execution all that is purposed and called for, in spite of opposition.*"

Carry through in action, carry through in prayer. There are times when our prayer is meant to be the kind of which St. Paul speaks in Philippians 4:6: "Be anxious for nothing, but in everything by prayer and supplication, with thanksgiving, let your requests be made known to God" (NKJV). To that the immediate answer is peace; but he speaks too of another kind of prayer, a labor, a conflict with dark powers, an agony. What do we know of that? What do *I* know of it?

❖   Ever since January 1905 there has been a monthly prayer day in Dohnavur. Once Amma was asked, "Why do we have a prayer day?" She replied:

Prayer Day

Why do we have a prayer day? I found one answer in a book called *The Principles of War*. It speaks of acting in the pressure of the most difficult circumstances, of "understanding and combining in order to obey." It talks of coordination and the keeping back of nothing: "All guns must be brought up, nothing must be kept in reserve." It says that victory will always be "a victory for all. It sometimes arises from the apparently fruitless efforts of some, but in every case from the concord between different arms, from the result of their converging efforts, from an assault delivered arm in arm" (Marshall Foch).

Wisdom and courage which no pressure of difficult circumstances can affect; understanding of our Lord's will and the power to combine with others so that His will may be done; the full surrender of all we have to give (this demands an utter denial of the *I* which likes best to do that which does not appear fruitless); the loyal love that results in concord—how are we to be trained and disciplined in this sort of warfare unless we spend time together in the presence of our Commander-in-Chief, learning from Him more and more perfectly the principles of war?

The Plan

The plan of our prayer day used to be this: It began at 9 a.m. and went on till 5 p.m. Alone or together, we were uninterrupted by meals or any other thing. We were far too much in earnest to wish for interruption. A burning sense of need was upon us.

We needed everything—most of all His presence ("If Your Presence does not go with us, do not bring us up from here"

Exod. 33:15, NKJV), for all was new, untracked, difficult.

Help we needed sorely too; helpers, for we were at the end of our strength often; money, for we had very little. We had to ask for miracles. Miracles can't be rushed.

As the children came we had to shorten the time of uninterrupted quiet. But the morning hours of work, and the short, very quiet mealtime some required after a full morning, were used as sacredly as the afternoon. These hours were devoted to the purpose of the day. There was an inward hush upon them.

We noticed that if ever we slipped into a careless keeping of these morning hours, or let ourselves fritter away any part of the afternoon, there was distinct loss. The life of the month lost in depth.

ANSWERS TO PRAYER

❖   Amma's whole life and work demonstrated the fact that God answers prayer. If He didn't, her life and work would have been impossible.

Here are just a few of many hundreds of examples she gave of answered prayer:

On Her Birthday

A lovely thing happened on my birthday, December 16th. I was sad that day, deep in my heart. The thought of one who had left us in foolish willfulness and made a most unhappy marriage was with me all the time, and I was anxious both about her and her little son. I had no way of finding her, for she had wandered away from our district and her husband had deserted her. The last two lines of our prayer for the children kept on singing through my soul,

> And wherever they may bide,
> Bring them home at eventide.

"Lord, find her, or lead me somehow to her," I prayed, "and for the sake of the little boy, long before eventide."

On the last day of the year suddenly that girl, Tamarai, walked into my room with her boy in her arms—such a bright little two-year-old with big sparkling eyes, who smiled up in my face.

"Tamarai!" I exclaimed, "What brought you back?"

"One night I had a dream," she said. "My people had been trying to persuade me to go to Ceylon. God spoke to me and said, 'Go back to your Amma.' So I refused to go to Ceylon. I told them of my dream and I have come."

"What night was it?" I asked her.

"It was the night of your birthday," she answered.

Her people would have respected and yielded to nothing short of the supernatural (such as a dream). So after all it was just what one should have expected to happen. There is nothing our God does not know about the limitations of souls and the perplexities of circumstances.

When things like this happen, one half turns around to see Him, like Mary in the garden (John 20:14). What will it be when we do see Him who has been with us all the time?

❖   Amma's children too learned that God answered their individual and secret prayers. This is how one of them received . . .

Victory Over Fear

When first we proposed a sail at Cape Comorin in a catamaran (three logs of well-seasoned wood, tied together at either end), Jeya did not want to go. She was afraid. Then she felt sorry for being afraid and she prayed, "Lord, give me victory over this fear. The sea is in the hollow of Your hand. Why should I fear to go for a sail in the hollow of Your hand? Take all the fear away!"

And He took the fear away.

Then she prayed, "Lord, when we go, if there is danger take care of us, and if there is no danger show me Your love on the sea."

She said, "When I saw the waves roll and fall over, my heart began to shake, but still I felt strong to go." I thought, "This is just the very time to show out the strength of God." If I sat still and did not fear when the sea was smooth, you would only be *a little* surprised. But if I sat still and did not fear when it was rough, you would be very much surprised, and you would know it was not my courage, no, not in the least measure, but the courage of Jesus who was brave in me. So I thought it would be a more shining answer if I came and was not afraid. I thought perhaps God had made the wind blow to give me an opportunity."

We were all sitting on the log edge, thinking not a thought of danger, when suddenly a great wave swept all six of us into the sea.

"I was enjoying everything when the big wave came," Jeya said. "I don't remember it throwing me out, but I felt my head go under the water. Then I remember coming up and seeing a rope high over my head, and I tried to catch it with my hand, but it moved up, and I went down. Then when I looked up again I saw it had moved down very low towards me, and I knew that God had moved it down, and I caught it with my hands.

"Then I saw that all the sisters were in the water too. But no fear came to me. No, not even the least little fear. God held the fear away. Then the next thing I know is somebody pulled me into the boat, and we sang and praised!"

She did not want to give up and go back, after that startling beginning. She and they all voted for going on.

"I wanted to see His strength shine out," she explained afterwards. "Oh, was it not good that we went through the storm! Now we have seen His power and His love, not only on the land, but also on the sea!"

❖ Again and again Amma found that prayer made all the difference. Long before any special meetings took place there would be regular prayer meetings in which the Holy Spirit's power was sought. Every detail, every individual, every possibility would be brought to God in earnest, expectant prayer. Often faith was tested, and it was not till the eleventh hour that the fruit of such prayer was seen.

The Last Meeting for Men

It was a solemn time. All through the week the influences generated by the weeks of prayer beforehand were moving upon those men as they sat in silent listening rows. But the inertia of the whole church was upon them too, and all who spoke felt the dead weight of that spiritual torpor. Sometimes it was as if they spoke to a stone wall.

But prayer has a working power, a penetrating power. The prayer of faith is not a vain thing, and the Lord's messengers did, at last, see Him break through and save some who to human hope were past saving. In the following-up work which will be going on we believe to see much more.

PROVISIONS

❖ Even before she left England, Amma had learned to depend on the Lord alone for the supply of all her needs and the needs of the work He entrusted to her. She never swerved from this principle of faith. She accepted that others were led differently, but for her it was a matter of obedience to a pattern shown her by her Lord.

As the family grew and its work expanded, no money was ever accepted from the government, and no appeals were made for funds. Several of Amma's books told the story of God's faithfulness in sending the money required, but she never wrote of a need till *after* it had been met.

To the people of the countryside, looking on and working out as best they could the cost of feeding, clothing, housing and educating her big family, it was a clear testimony to the faithfulness of the one true and living God. To this day all who work for the fellowship know their bills will be paid promptly, and that no loan is ever accepted or debt incurred.

It is not an easy position to maintain. Amma wrote:

Finance

Are we asking for too much? But is God poor? He whose city streets are paved with gold (Rev. 21:21), cannot He give us not spoonfuls only, of the dust of these streets, but handfuls too? I love the symbol of those streets—gold underfoot, just where it should be.

So long as the word is in the Bible, "It is NOT the will of your Father that one of these little ones should perish," so long surely must we continue to save children, and therefore we shall have gold enough to save them.

Vision

We need to walk very carefully lest we make any mistake and commit our God to send us supplies to do something He has not commanded. We have no right to do this, for there is no promise that says He will hold Himself responsible for an uncommanded thing.

"For a web begun God finds the thread," if in very truth He, not we, began it. So the real crux must be to find the answer to the question, "Lord, is it You who command me, or only my own desire?" And then later, "Is this work being carried on according to Your pattern, and Yours only?"

I don't think we can ever count on thread being supplied for a pattern He has not planned. Our prayer must be, "Protect me from mistaking my desire for Your direction."

So we need vision. There is nothing to hinder anyone from receiving vision, if the will be set on obedience. But anything coming between the Lord and us, any faltering in obedience, any compromise, and the vision is blurred.

This is a very serious thing. "Where there is no vision the people perish" (Prov. 29:18).

Ask, Seek, Knock

Many an hour, many a night has been spent in what our forefathers in England called the *exercise* of prayer—sometimes difficult exercise, sometimes painful too. And work lay behind that exercise, much writing to win prayer for the children of whose very existence few had ever heard; many journeys, many earnest talks. For it is not in God's plan that money should drop like rain from the skies. It is not thus that He answers prayer. It is ask, seek, knock (Matt. 7:7).

"My God shall supply all your need according to his riches" (Phil. 4:19). We lay those words before our Lord and we say to Him very earnestly, "And now, O Lord, do as You have said."

❖ Often Amma was comforted and strengthened through some passage in a book she was reading, for even in her ordinary reading she was always alert to hear what God had to say to her. She found "figures of the true" in the most unlikely places, including a factory in America.

Feather and Bar

In America there is a factory where one of the processes has to do with the cooling and carrying of certain substances by air blown through fine slits in a trough.

A feather was placed at one end of this grid-like trough, and it was blown softly by the current of air which rose from beneath and carried to the other end of the trough.

Then a piece of iron, four inches wide, an inch thick and eight feet long, was put in. "And the wings of the wind carried it as simply and easily the whole length of the trough as they had carried the feather."

I looked up as I read it and said aloud, "Thank You, my dear Father."

In January 1904 the work, which was then evangelistic only, required five pounds and six shillings a month. What a feather it looks like today! Now it feels simply tremendous, a bar of iron indeed.

But the power which floated the feather floated the bar. Just think of it—feather and bar, all one to the Wind.

❖ Sometimes God spoke to her in dreams, as He did once at a time of special financial need. But even in her dreams it was God's own words which helped her, as in this case when He spoke through 1 Peter 5:7 and Matthew 6:8:

A Dream

One night I had been awake for a long time thinking and praying. It was a lovely still night lit by a young moon, and I looked at the mountains lying in the moonlight and then at the nurseries in the big garden—a dream of quiet loveliness. Everything looked so untroubled, unanxious.

"But, Lord, the children cannot live on moonlight," I found myself saying; and the answer came back so gently,

"Yes, I know."

Then I remembered the many whose love would do so much more if only they could. I thought too of those passed into fuller life [in heaven], where though they may walk on golden pavements, they cannot send one little handful of its gold down to us here. All these thoughts went into that familiar talk with the unseen Companion (who is so much nearer than the nearest seen), till at last I went back to bed and to sleep, comforted.

And then I seemed to be in a great bank. I thought it was Barclays Bank. I saw the broad polished counter and all the paraphernalia of a bank at home. I looked up, and saw running around the wall in a kind of frieze these words:

CASTING ALL YOUR CARE UPON HIM FOR HE CARES FOR YOU. YOUR HEAVENLY FATHER KNOWS THAT YOU HAVE NEED OF ALL THESE THINGS.

"How good to know Barclays Bank is like this!" I said, and I thought of all the poor troubled people who must go in and look up and find consolation.

Then I began to wonder if it really was an earthly bank; but did they have banks in heaven? And with that I woke, not very willingly, for I did not want to leave that very pleasant place.

Nor have I ever left it since, for a new confidence and comfort and peace seemed to come then and there. When little tormenting voices say, "The people at home will never understand about the exchange rate," or "You may be thankful if you are just able to carry on. Don't expect to break new ground," then I turn and see the door of Barclays Bank standing wide open, and I run in and look up at the frieze. And the little weary, despondent, faithless voices stay outside.

But the end of the dream? A few days later, "*He cares for you*," were the words written across an envelope in which I found a check. In another gift-letter came the words, "*Your heavenly Father knows that you have need of all these things*."

❖ Just a dream? A very practical one, for all through the years (more than eighty-five years now) those two verses have been fulfilled again and again. God's promises are eternal and they never fail.

No one in Dohnavur receives a salary, though as in a family all needs are met. Indeed it was and is a *family*, and everyone shares their possessions. Those from overseas who have private means pay for their living expenses. Some receive what they need direct from the Lord; others equally directly from the Lord through the shared resources of the fellowship.

In answer to a question from one of the Indian workers Amma wrote her thoughts about money:

The Stewardship of Money

In Old Testament days it was understood that one tenth of all possessions belonged to God, and only anything that was over and above the tenth was a gift, a freewill offering. Many go by this rule now.

Often a word spoken by our Lord turns a clear light on practical things, for example, Luke 12:15: "One's life does not consist in the abundance of the things he possesses" (NKJV).

This is the exact opposite of the world's thought. But "Sell what you have and give," verse 33, was not spoken to all then, nor is it spoken to all Christians now. It was not spoken to the twelve disciples. They had left all and had nothing to sell. They had given their lives and their love, and that gift was the dearest of all to their Lord. It was spoken to those of His disciples to whom verse 22 was spoken, "Do not worry about your life . . ." (NKJV) and also, Wesley thinks, to the 120 mentioned in Acts 1:15 and to the Seventy, that they like the Twelve might be free from all earthly entanglements.

Later His word was different, Luke 22:36: "He who has a money bag, let him take it, and likewise a knapsack" (NKJV), as if to say, "if you can pay your expenses yourself, certainly do so."

Some of us are like Peter, "Silver and gold have I none." But we have other things: for example, books. Am I sharing my books and what I read in them? Am I sharing every joy I can?

But the simplest way to think of the matter is this: "I am Yours and all I have is Yours. Lord, do as You will with me and with all that I call mine."

Nothing Too Precious

What a difference it makes when people give "not grudgingly or of necessity" (2 Cor. 9:7) but loving their Lord and His cause enough to give Him that which they would naturally want for themselves! I turn again and again to the word which says, "If thou bestow on the hungry that which thy soul desireth . . . THEN the Lord shall satisfy thy soul in dry places" (Isa. 58:10–11, RV margin).

When they see Him whom their souls love, will they regret they had in very truth "nothing too precious for Jesus"?

Basket

5

Praise, Not Depression

❖ To Amma, praise was as essential a part of life as prayer. Failure to praise was tantamount to treachery, for it meant refusal to accept that the will of God was "good, acceptable and perfect" (Rom. 12:2). However grim the circumstances, she herself expressed her implicit trust in the love and power of her Lord by praising Him and encouraging others to do likewise.

Sing Your Glad Doxology

Let the hosts of darkness shout;
    Let them rage and roar;
Christ will put them all to rout
    As He did before.
      Praise Him,
      Praise Him,
    Praise Him heartily;
    Sing your glad Doxology.

See you shall, for He is God;
    Praise prepares His way.
Feet that on the sea have trod
    Tread the waves today.

> Praise Him,
> Praise Him,
> Praise Him joyously;
> Sing your glad Doxology.

Sing your glad Doxology, don't just say it. Sing it forth. "Before the gods I will sing praises to you" (Psalm 138:1, NKJV).

When I was learning Tamil and understood very little of the service and nothing of the sermon, the recurrent Doxology after the Psalms used to thrill me.

> Glory be to the Father and to the Son and to the Holy Ghost,
> *As it was in the beginning,*
> *Is now*
> *And ever shall be*
> *World without end, Amen.*

There is more blue than grey in the sky (in India at least!). Don't be preoccupied with the grey, look at the blue. Show the blue. Sing your glad Doxology.

The Doxology stands like a great eternal mountain and will stand when the drifting mists of time are utterly forgotten. "Satan, thy kingdom hath suffered loss," wrote brave John Wesley over two hundred years ago. "Thou fool! How long wilt thou contend with Him that is mightier than thou?"

Christ Is Conqueror

"Christ is Conqueror. Amen. Hallelujah!" Long ago in Japan those words were worked on a banner for me by a friend. I put it up on my wall in Bangalore and kept it there till it was devoured by poochies, the hungry insect tribe of India. But poochies cannot get into one's heart, and it hangs there still.

❖ Amma was only human and she was often sorely tried, but she always ended up singing, as the following extract shows:

The Messengers

2 Corinthians 12:7	A messenger of Satan to buffet.
Job 28:3	He setteth an end.
Psalm 42:8	In the night His song.
Job 35:10	Who gives songs in the night.

Last night in Job I read the story of the four messengers. There were just four, then no more came. God set an end to the darkness that had been allowed for so long.

A few weeks ago we counted four messengers and hoped there was not a fifth around the next corner. But there was, and just for a minute we found ourselves very much wishing he wasn't there. But soon we saw what a chance was being given us to disappoint the devil and glorify our Lord.

What I want to make sure of now is that as messenger after messenger comes from Satan to buffet us, he goes back to his master baffled because he found us singing.

Oh that I could sing it all over the world: We have a good Father! It is absolutely safe to trust Him. We may fail, our faith may fail—mine has many a time, and I have had to go to Him desperately for a renewal of it—but He remains faithful: He cannot deny Himself (2 Tim. 2:13, NKJV).

The Ministry Is Praise

I have been thinking so much lately about the old Jewish legend that the angels only lived as they ministered. "They are renewed every morning," said the Rabbis, "and after they have praised God, they return to the Stream of Fire out of which they came."

Is it not a wonderful conception? We only live as we minister, and the ministry is praise. "Who makes his angels spirits and his ministers a flame of fire" (Heb. 1:7, NKJV). Are we cool? Or cooling? Let us go back to the Stream of Fire, and then renewed and reinspired go forth to burn with the love of God that is "as a very flame." Nothing less is sufficient to burn the iciness out of us. We must bathe afresh in the shining Stream if we are to burn and shine.

Sing a New Song

When our Lord told us to consider the flowers and the birds, He may have had more in mind than just their freedom from care. Think of the joy of the birds in the morning; think of the dawn chorus.

Surely our days too should begin with song. God forgive us for every songless morning. Who should sing if we do not? For the Lord has redeemed us and ransomed us from the hand of one stronger than us. Therefore let us come and sing and flow together to the goodness of the Lord (Jer. 31:11–12).

❖   There were many occasions when things seemed to go wrong. Babies saved after much toil, and nursed devotedly, died. Workers came—and went. False stories were spread around and believed. Illness struck down those whom it seemed impossible to spare. Lawsuits were lost.

Through it all Amma clung to her faith in the sovereignty of God.

His Eternal Purpose

"Him, being delivered by the determinate counsel and fore-knowledge of God. . . ." Dr. Campbell Morgan in his *Acts* says that the word in chapter 2:23 translated "determinate" is the word from which we derive our word "horizon." All that happened to our Lord Jesus was "within the boundaries of His purpose."

And we have the letter to the Ephesians to tell us that as it was with the blessed Son of God, so it is even with us. "In Him also we have obtained an inheritance, being predestined according to the purpose of Him who works all things according to the counsel of His will, that we should be to the praise of His glory" (Eph. 1:11–12, NKJV).

All that can ever happen is within the boundaries of our Father's purpose—His eternal purpose. With this horizon-thought in mind, it is simply reasonable and right never to be disappointed but to praise.

❖ Amma often quoted Psalm 50:23 (RV margin): "Whoso offereth the sacrifice of thanksgiving glorifieth me; and prepareth a way that I may show him the salvation of God." She believed praise did indeed lead to God's victory and His glory.

Ambushes

"Now when they began to sing and to praise, the Lord set ambushes against the children of Ammon . . . and they were defeated" (2 Chron. 20:21–22, NKJV).

Let us go out before the army and say, "Praise the Lord; for

His mercy endures forever." Then surely it will be as it was long ago, and when we begin to sing and to praise, the Lord will set ambushes and the foe will be smitten. There will be spoil, more than we can carry away, abundance, both riches and precious jewels, to lay at His feet at the end of the day.

For Good

"Ye meant evil against me, but God meant it for good" (Gen. 50:20, RV). "All things work together for good." (Rom. 8:23).

> The foe meant thine ill,
> The Father, thy blessing;
> Always 'tis so.
> O heart, be thou still,
> However distressing
> Sharp winds that blow.
>
> The Seen and Unseen,
> The stars in their courses,
> All own His sway;
> His powers intervene,
> His heavenly forces
> Compass our day.
>
> If truly all things
> Are working together
> Only for good,
> The trusting heart sings,
> Whatever the weather.
> Beatitude.

NOT DEPRESSION

❖ Amma's life was "hidden with Christ in God" (Col. 3:3), but just as her Lord suffered being tempted, so did she. Those who went to her for help always found that she could understand their temptations and trials because she had experienced them herself, usually at a far deeper level. She sought to encourage and comfort others with the comfort with which she herself had been comforted by God (2 Cor. 1:4).

Disappointment

The disciple is not above his Master, nor the servant above his Lord (Matt. 10:24). Our Lord Jesus went further on the path of disappointment and grief than ever we have gone. His servant Paul followed Him there, and who are we that we should not walk in that painful path?

Whatever the pressure, there is always something to waken a song. "Let the hearts of those rejoice who seek the Lord" (Ps. 105:3, NKJV).

And yet though we believe all this and have often proved it true, sometimes it is as if the devil set himself to depress the heart that does truly desire to rejoice. And this depression can befog a whole community. They go on with the work as usual, but there isn't a lifting joy. Prayer meetings go on, but they are sticky.

At such times the only thing is for each one individually, and all together as a company, resolutely to look up to the Lord, though it be through the fog. "O give me the comfort of thy help again and establish me with thy free spirit" (Ps. 51:12, BCP). "They looked to Him and were radiant, and their faces were not ashamed" (Ps. 34:5, NKJV).

The one deadly thing is a dull contentment in the fog.

Crying for Nothing

A few evenings ago little three-year-old Compassion was crying softly to herself, and when her *Accal* asked her why she was crying she said, "I am crying for nothing, nothing at all!"

Her *Accal* understood, and took her in her arms and carried her out to the verandah and said, "Look at the moon." It was a cloudy night and many black clouds were chasing across the face of the moon.

"See," said her *Accal*, "the clouds cover the moon's face sometimes, but they pass and she shines like silver. She isn't crying, though the clouds are in the sky."

Then Compassion looked and looked. "Not at me did she look," said her *Accal*, "but just with her little face held up she looked at the moon, the bright silver moon. And ever since, when she has been tempted to be unhappy and cry I have said to her, 'Think of the moon!' and she has always laughed and forgotten to be sad."

Will this moon-story help anyone as it helped me? The clouds will pass. The moon will shine on, for the moon sees the sun.

Tempted to Look Back

I wonder, will it help anyone tempted to look back as I am often tempted, if I tell of this afternoon?

First came, as distinctly as if a voice had spoken aloud,

> Thy day is almost done,
> How few the victories won,
> How slow thy crawl, thou who didst hope to fly!

Thou who hast often told
Of shining heavenly gold
How grey thine evening sky!
Why art thou thus, merely a cumberer?
Was ever broken vessel emptier?

Just before that I had been reading Conybeare's translation of Ephesians 5:19, so I could only answer:

Be still, mine enemy;
I hear another word:
"Make melody
With music of the heart
Unto thy Lord."

But I had no melody. How does one make melody unless one is given the music? So I asked for a song, and a tiny thing came—too simple perhaps to write—and yet it says what I want to say.

An empty shell lay by the sea;
The waves rolled up, and all forgot
To think of that which mattered not;
They only saw the sea.

So be it, Lord; let this Thy shell
Be lost in glory of the sea;
And as the waves sweep over me,
Let all forget the shell.

No Roof

"Believe under a cloud, and wait for Him when there is no moonlight nor starlight." Samuel Rutherford wrote this in 1640; and the words are good for us all to store up in memory, for we never know when we shall be trusted to walk without moonlight or starlight.

"By his Spirit he adorned the heavens" (Job 26:13). I pass the word on to any of you who seem to be walled about by trial or limitations of any sort, or by pain. There may be walls around our room of life, but there is never a roof overhead. No power on earth can put up that roof, for above us are the heavens adorned with stars.

Depression Defeated

One of our Indian fellow-workers was depressed and needed help, so he stayed for a while in the hospital, and his various ills were relieved and his heart comforted. He was reminded of the blessing that came to Job when he helped others.

Just then there was a man who came in great trouble to the hospital and was welcomed and treated, and given a New Testament to read. That night he could not sleep, "not because of pain, but because of joy." Never before had he read such words. He read and read. He read 123 pages and then laid the book down, open on his bed.

Meanwhile, the aforetime discouraged but now restored one had been asking for a message to give the patient. "Read Acts 16." He was sure that was what the heavenly voice was saying. So he went to the ward where the man was and told him so.

"That is just where I left off!" said the man, much surprised, and he showed him the New Testament open on the bed at Acts 16. He knew then that there was Someone whom neither he nor his new friend could see but who saw them, saw him, saw even the page where he had stopped reading. From this point he went on, until now he is truly the Lord's.

"You comprehend my path and my lying down, and are acquainted with all my ways. Such knowledge is too wonderful for me" (Ps. 139:3, 6, NKJV). How vivid, how true to this common day the words of our Bible are.

❖ Some of Amma's messages were written specially for her young children, and then she often used illustrations from nature to help them understand. All the children had watched the family of kingfishers of which she wrote in this note:

Don't Give Up

The younger of the baby kingfishers has caught his first fish. He flew off with it to show it to his mother. We heard all she said about it, and all he said. Mother and son have talked of nothing else for the last ten minutes.

But just before this joy the young kingfisher had a great disappointment. He had been practising all kinds of dives, and at last he came up jubilant. He had a beakful of something! He could hardly stand for excitement—but it wasn't a fish. It was a leaf.

Have you ever felt as I think that poor little bird felt then? (It took him quite a long time to recover from his disappointment.) You thought you had found power and patience to deal with some difficulty, and then somehow you hadn't. Leaf for fish—it was rather like that.

Then do what the kingfisher did. Don't give up. Seek again. "In due season we shall reap if we do not lose heart" (Gal. 6:9, NKJV). "He also taught them by a parable that they must always pray and never lose heart" (Luke 18:1, Weymouth).

❖ Amma enjoyed her children and they enjoyed her. Life was never dull while she was around. Even the village children seemed irresistibly attracted to her, so much so that she was called in Tamil "the child-catching lady." Some thought she had some power to bewitch children. The secret, of course, was her love.

She delighted in her children's questions and comments, often writing about them to the friends whose prayers she coveted.

Mountains

The girls were tremendously impressed by the mountains and most of all by the thought that God had created them ready-made, so to speak. They had always thought they *grew*!

They chattered away to each other. "Trees grow from little plants; they are not big all at once. But mountains! Just think of them being so big from the first!"

One day I found Victory standing meditatively on a smooth low rock. "See!" she said, "There is a rock just like this at Palayamkottai. I always thought it was growing slowly into a big rock, and that at last it would be a mountain, but now I look at these mountains—so big all at once—and I think of God's great, *great* power, and oh! I am glad He is my God!"

❖ Amma's heart echoed that comment, for it was her relationship with God that mattered most. In Him, and in Him alone, she found all that she needed. She did not always understand, but she always trusted and so was satisfied.

Satisfied

It has been a great comfort to me to realize anew that it is God and only God we need. "Thou, O Lord, art the Thing that I long for" (Psalm 71:5, BCP).

Yes, it is He, our Lord, our Beloved, who satisfies our heart and makes us whole and strong however pressed the outward man may be.

Our God DOES satisfy. I think sometimes He has to draw us into strange experiences in order that we shall prove Him to the uttermost, for some purpose out of sight. For what is He preparing us? It is all hidden; we have only hints, such as "His servants shall serve Him" (Rev. 22:3)—where? how?

But this we do know: never a pang of disappointment or loneliness or pain (and there are many different kinds of pangs) but may be turned to minister towards a perfecting of power to serve—first here, then Otherwhere.

We do not know the answers to the hard questions of life, but we know our Lord, we love Him, we trust Him, we do not wish to trouble Him with questions. Why should we?

Basket

6

Healing

❖ In the early days Amma had no doctor or medical staff to help her. The babies who were saved were often tiny and delicate (they still are), and for a while she had a nursery for the babies at the London Missionary Society hospital in Neyoor, some miles from Dohnavur. Ponnammal (whose story is told in the book of that name) was in charge there.

For many years she depended on this hospital for help, and Dr. Pugh frequently visited Dohnavur to examine those who were ill. Some who needed surgery went to the Neyoor Hospital.

Amma described what happened on one such occasion:

Operation Successful

We had a glorious day here—prayer all day in the Prayer Room, one set after another praying without a break. Then at 3 p.m. came the wire, "Operation successful. No cancer."

The whole place went mad with joy. There was lots of dancing before the Lord and a big thanksgiving service in the evening. Everybody was singing "O God of Stars":

O God of stars and flowers, forgive our blindness;
　　No dream of night had dared what Thou hast wrought!
New every morning is Thy lovingkindness,
　　Far, far above what we have asked or thought.

So, under every sky, our "Alleluia,"
　　With flowers of morning and with stars of night,
Shall praise Thee, O Lord Jesus—Alleluia—
　　Till Thou shalt fold all shadows up in light.

Wings 11

❖　But before this, in 1922, a little book called *The Healing of Christ in His Church* was sent to Amma. Its impact was enormous. Amma wrote in her home letter that August:

Community-Faith

One sentence in that book struck me as if written just for Dohnavur. "If community-faith were far stronger and more widely diffused, we can but think that works of healing would be much more seen and much more widely spread. In a world of real Christian faith, the non-healing of disease would be more remarkable than is healing."

Surely, if anywhere community-faith could be possible, it should be possible here and now in Dohnavur? A sentence on a previous page had arrested me: "I believe that our Lord is coming very near to His people at this present time, and that we may thankfully and reverently be waiting to receive Him. It is my humble and solemn conviction that the awakening to the truth of the spiritual healing which is being manifested not only all around us here but also in isolated and distant countries at this time—that this awakening is the call of Christ the Bridegroom to His Bride the Church; and it is a most wonderful manifestation of His love."

The book, with its humble reverent way of touching on the subject, was helpful. Here there was no ranting, no vulgar cock-sureness, no pretending that what wasn't *was*, no putting the ministry of doctors and nurses outside the pale. I had found it, till now, impossible to come to any clear conclusion about healing. Now I could and did.

Looking back on only a few weeks, I saw how God's leading had been most gently but quite definitely in this direction. Instead of praying alone or in a general way for thirteen-year-old Thai who was ill, I had felt moved to take to the hospital a group on whom I could count for special cooperation; and we had prayed. Thai, who for a whole month had been running an evening temperature of *103°* or *102°*, was normal next evening, and it never rose again. Was it, that definite healing, a light on the path, an insistent encouraging, "Fear not. Go on"?

But the thousand pitfalls! If only someone who knew the way were there! And then and there, as I stood with the book in my hand, it was as if the word were spoken by one present in the room, "Am *I* not here?"

Rukma's Healing

From this time on a careful medical record has been kept of all who were brought for healing, so that it will be possible to know just what is and is not being done. We see not only what happens at the time, as in a passing mission, but afterwards.

I will tell briefly something of what has been going on since the word came, "Am *I* not here?"

Rukma had a very painful trouble with her forefinger, and Dr. Pugh had operated once. The finger was healing when she struck it by accident; the pain returned and neuritis set in the arm. She felt she had gone under rather badly during those weeks of strain and the distress of a horrible-looking finger, which she could not believe would ever be of use again. She thought perhaps she was going to be given a second chance to glorify her Master where she had rather sadly failed. Many feared Dr. Pugh would say, when he examined it, that it must come off to the first joint.

Rukma came humbly that morning, asking for pardon for the failure of the past and courage and willingness to go through with it, and then we prayed.

It was a very solemn moment. The pain was all the way up the arm. Rukma, worn down by her difficult weeks, was a shadow of herself and looked tired out. The time was our usual prayer time when all the household who can, gather for worship. What would happen? We rose from our knees not knowing what had happened.

Half-an-hour afterwards the pain had gone from the arm; next day it passed completely from the finger. No one will ever forget the solemn joy of that experience.

But the doctor? Would he feel it safe to leave it? He came soon afterwards to see another patient, so he examined the finger. There was a little tenderness on the top of the bone where he had taken away the dead part. Otherwise it was all right. Nothing more need be done.

"Is it *really* all right?" I asked.

"Yes," he said, glancing up, I expect surprised; but it was rather momentous to Rukma and me. And though we kept quite quiet, we both sang a little "Jubilate" as he repeated that it was quite all right.

Babies Healed

Next day three little babies, wrapped in white shawls, were brought (and healed). And so it has gone on ever since.

One day a Hindu sub-magistrate happened to call at prayer time. That morning a baby boy was brought so that we might give thanks for his healing, and little Thai also stood up before all to thank our Lord for hers. The feel of the room was very joyful indeed. It impressed the sub-magistrate immensely.

"I did not know that anywhere the Lord Jesus Christ was doing these things now," was his remark. He had heard of the healings and had attributed them to autosuggestion; but when he heard of the babies being healed he was dumb. Autosuggestions a potent force in certain troubles, was impotent here.

"No, it is not that; it cannot be that with infants," he said.

Always on such days we sing something specially happy, like . . .

> Consecrated to Thy glory
> I will live and die to Thee,
> I will witness to Thy glory
> Of salvation full and free.

Its roof-lifting chorus is very fine in its Tamil translation.

Mystery

Days when any are brought for healing are very still and solemn. Next to prayer for spiritual healing, it is the most intense thing I know, thus openly, definitely, to bring the sick to our holy, our very present Lord. There is always the sense of mystery about it, for sometimes it quite evidently is His wish to heal otherwise; and sometimes there is no healing on earth.

One dear little child with a diseased heart is waiting to be taken. And yet, "An enemy has done this"(Matt. 13:23, NKJV) is and always has been my one word where disease and pain are concerned. When Christ was on earth He always healed, and almost always instantly. Why not always now? Why not always instantly?

So it is with no light assurance that we come; I do not know anything more solemn and full of awe than these times.

Old Sundarie and Blessing

Sometimes the awe breaks into laughter. Never shall we forget the Sunday when Sundarie, an invaluable old servant, came with another servant to return thanks for her healing.

She had come to me on the previous Thursday, eager and trembling, and had seized my hands.

"Amma, lay your hands upon me. Oh, touch me with your hands!"

I had told her as clearly as ever I could that it was not my touch but our Lord Jesus that healed. But she had insisted, and gently drawing my hands over her shoulder and arm had said, "O Lord, touch me too!"

I had got her to come to prayers, and on that same day, Blessing, the young gardener, came too, and he and she, both true Christians, were indeed touched that very hour. So on Sunday they came to give thanks.

Blessing is a young man of twenty, who was swept down by the river in the forest when the other man was drowned. While he was in the foaming water, he was saved in soul and immediately after in body; for a tree, past which he was being swept, leaned its branches over the river, and he caught them and dragged himself out.

❖   Often when someone long-prayed-for died, apparently unconverted, Amma would quote the lines:

> Betwixt the saddle and the ground
> He mercy sought, he mercy found.

Blessing's conversion, at the very moment when he expected to drown in the flash flood as his companion did, was a wonderful proof that this could indeed happen.

Blessing stood up now and told how in the very moment of prayer he knew himself well. He was bent with, I suppose, lumbago. We have no doctor to tell us what is wrong, so can only suppose. Anyhow he could not work, and as he is the support of his family, it is serious for them all when he is ill.

Then Sundarie, whose shoulder had been swollen with rheumatism, held out her skinny old arm.

"Look at it!" she exclaimed, waggling it vigorously. "Look at it!" And I need not say we did.

"It was swollen, it was full of pain. I could not do my work. I came to Amma." And she said what she had said to me and I to her—then, seizing my hand, went through it all in most vivid pantomime while the children stared, fascinated.

"Ah, but it was swollen! My shoulder was like this," and she indicated a lump the size of a small turnip. "You know I came to prayers and of the prayer for its healing. That very hour it went down so much" (showing how much). "I pounded my rice" (more gestures), "and half the pain went, three quarters went. See, it is quite well" (and she stretched it out); "but there is still a trifle of pain in it, to the Lord be praise!"

This last was just too much. The whole room broke into laughter. Old Sundarie laughed, we all laughed.

Jullanie

Once again I heard that kind of laughter, this time in the room leading into the operating room of the Neyoor hospital. Jullanie had for several years been ill. When Dr. Pugh examined her, he found things so distinctly wrong that he said she must come to Neyoor hospital.

Now Jullanie is greatly needed. She felt it was her Lord's intention to heal her *here*, and we prayed.

Well, she was healed. It is a little thing to write, but it was *not* a little thing. It was so dangerous to make any mistake about it that Dr. Pugh felt he would like to examine her.

I glanced from her face to his as he was doing it.

"No pain?" and he pressed over the previously sensitive place. "None at all?" He pressed deeper, searched most carefully, found nothing.

"Can you take your rice and curry now? Three good square meals a day?"

"Yes, I can!" came most confidently up from the table. (She had lived on bread soaked in milk for a year.)

"Are you hungry?"

"Yes, very!"

Then he laughed. And, prone as she was on the table, Jullanie laughed. It was perfectly delightful. We all laughed!

I know there are hysterical conditions which simulate nearly everything, but I don't think anyone who really knew Jullanie thought this was her trouble. Anyhow here she was, *well*, and Dr. Pugh was as pleased as we were. She came back to Dohnavur and there was another glad quarter of an hour in the Room of Praise.

The Healer

When I had to leave home on business, some thought the healings would cease. But I was glad to have the chance to prove to all who the Healer was. When I left, Arulai led at prayers, backed up by the whole family.

There was only one couple who dropped out. Some people from the Dohnavur village had a child with hip disease, and I had asked them to come to prayers so that they might understand things better. When they saw Arulai in my place, they were not pleased and did not come again.

"So it was not God they were looking at" was the children's true comment.

A new baby was sent to us, a lovely little Brahman boy of ten days or so. He developed water on the knee and a swollen foot, and of course a high temperature. He was far too ill to be taken to Neyoor hospital. He could not have borne the shaking in the bullock cart.

After prayer—the prayer of the whole family—his temperature fell and he slept. Yesterday for the first time he moved his little leg almost straight out. He is not perfectly healed yet. One waits, not knowing with any easy assurance what the will of the Lord is, but longing for the very touch that was of old, the touch that perfectly restored at once. Why is it not so now?

Is this sentence, which is often in my mind, the answer to that question? "We must remember in contrite humility that the way of healing is like a broken, long-disused road—it is overgrown with the thorns and briers of our long neglect; it is blocked with the boulders of thoughts and ways of the world that are not the thoughts and ways of God. The bridges of faith have been half broken, the gates of prayer have been too often closed. Should we dare to ask or expect our Lord to come in healing and to do His mighty works among us, as though the way were made straight for His feet?"

Sometimes I wonder if even we of Dohnavur may be allowed to roll just one small boulder out of the way, that the path may be by just so much the straighter for His feet.

Manoharam

All the time these healings were happening, Manoharam lay in her prison-house of pain. Once it seemed as if the answer to our prayer for her was to be healing here and now, for there were two almost painless days. She thought so herself and was sadly disappointed when it proved otherwise. But we went to the Scriptures of comfort. John the Baptist's story seemed to run on almost parallel lines with hers. The word to him was not deliverance, but "Blessed is he who is not offended because of Me" (Luke 7:23, NKJV).

❖ Manoharam is still alive, still quietly serving the Lord in Dohnavur, aged 93! She finds it hard to wait for her home-call.

No one could have imagined that Manoharam, always delicate but always a spiritual warrior, would outlive all the others; but many thank God for all that her long life has meant to them.

The Greater Healing

Another thought has probably come to some: What of the greater healings of the spirit? Are they to be pushed aside as of less account?

We think they are of *more* account, and we cannot help wondering when any other healing, even for a moment, seems more important to anyone. We find sometimes it does. "Wonderful!" is the word as the eyes of the listener kindle over some happy story of healing; but when we tell of what counts for much *more* with us, we do not always find quite the same keen response.

But the perfectly splendid truth is that the one has greatly helped forward the other. After watching for several days, a little Hindu lad said to Arulai, "*Accal*, is it really as Amma said it might be yesterday? Will Jesus the Lord heal the sickness in my soul as He healed those little children's bodies?"

Arulai asked, "What is your sickness?" And he told her truthfully. So she knew he was ready, and next morning, after a quiet talk, he and two others knelt with us in the Room of Praise and asked for the touch that makes the spirit whole.

In the last tour (evangelizing in the villages) Edith was called in to pray for the sick, and as one might expect as one reads the Gospels, there were healings. In two or three cases the healings were so definite that the only wonder was that the whole household did not turn to the Lord! Perhaps our dear Lord sometimes heals just out of sheer love of being kind to poor people; we don't hear that all whom He healed long ago came to Him in truth.

I was put off these matters for years because I was not convinced they led to the definite saving of souls, and I feared being sidetracked. But as I think of the tender mercy of the Lord, I am not sure I was right. And may it not be, in ways out of our sight, that the witness of His love may draw souls of whom perhaps we shall never know, to taste and see that He is good? (Ps. 34:8).

Questions

Why do we need a doctor at all? I can only say I don't know. I don't know why our Lord Jesus does not come and heal *all* by His touch as He healed when He was on earth. But it would not be true to say He does. An aching tooth has to come out or it goes on aching. And so on, with more important things.

Since I last wrote some have been healed and some have not, and why some have and some have not I do not know. So far as one could see, the conditions were the same. Must it not be that there is more in this question than can be set forth in a clear-cut sentence? More of mystery? The secret things still belong to the Lord (Deut. 29:29). What children understand all their father does?

I am at rest, while I hope following on, for I feel sure our kind Lord is at least as eager to open His great reserves of blessing and of power as we are to enter into them, and will He not do it if we are willing? And do we not know Him well enough to be content not to understand?

The Fellowship of Joy

"That I may know him and the fellowship of his sufferings" (Phil. 3:10). There are many times in life when this is the one word for us, but sometimes we are called into the fellowship of His joy. I think there is more than even the very pure joy of seeing Him victorious over the enemy—"an enemy has done this" (Matt. 13:28); "whom Satan has bound for eighteen years" (Luke 13:16, NKJV). There is such a thing as humble *fellowship* in that joy.

Such a doctor as Dr. Pugh of Neyoor must know it many times, as his hand is used to lift one who was all but dead out of the grasp of death and set him free to serve. And each of us in our little measure, whether we minister towards the recovery of the sick by nursing or by prayer, or by both, are called I think into the fellowship. It is a quickening fellowship. Just as when He calls, "Rejoice with me over this sheep that was lost," so it is then. We look up into the Face that was more marred than any other (Isa. 52:14) and see it alight with joy.

It was of the Man of Sorrows the Father said, "Your God has anointed You with the oil of gladness more than Your companions" (Heb. 1:9, NKJV). Oh to live in the unbroken fellowship of these things!

❖   Although Amma's tender heart rejoiced as she saw pain relieved and the ill healed, it was not physical healing that mattered most to her, but spiritual. So she was not altogether happy about a conversation overheard in a bus after the first lady doctor had joined her, but before the Dohnavur hospital was built.

Two Hindu women were talking. One asked the other, "Where is that lady going?"

"Oh, to Dohnavur."

"In that place there is a doctor lady who listens to all you tell her about your illness and then answers you, and before she has finished answering you, you are quite well. And if you look behind her you see angels standing there!"

What a joy it would be (Amma commented) if healing could come as simply as that, and what a greater joy it would be if the people could see not the angels but the Lord of the angels, directing the service that is done in His name. But not so easily does any soul see the things of the Kingdom, the "must" of Calvary, the cross, the glory that was won through suffering.

❖ Then the healings ceased for a while. There were several reasons. One was that Amma herself became almost totally immersed in a battle for the souls of two notorious dacoits. This resulted in her being away from Dohnavur more than usual, and she found people did not bring their sick when she was away. In other words, they looked to *her* as healer, rather than the Lord.

Earlier, as a note in her diary told, she had definitely asked for a gift of healing and had received it. Now there was another note in her *Daily Light*: "Asked for the gift of healing for the sake of others," and she added, "Answer, 'No.'"

Instead she heard our Lord say very clearly, "My glory will I *not* give to another" (Isa. 42:8). She wrote:

God's Glory

God is not mocked. If a company or a soul yields to ambition or to any earthly aim whatever, God to whom alone all glory belongs and who will not give His glory to another, deals most solemnly with that company or soul.

The Dohnavur Fellowship exists only by His mercy. It will perish (and better it should perish) if it lets the love of praise creep in, or becomes cold in love, or in any way forgets that in all things He must have the preeminence (Col. 1:18). The Lord save us from this snare.

❖ But Amma could not ignore the pain and suffering she saw in the villages all around Dohnavur, and she and her companions began to pray for a hospital; a place of healing for soul as well as for body, and for doctors and nurses who would be first and foremost evangelists. Only such men and women could train Amma's children and lead them out into loving service to the sick.

These prayers were answered, though it was not till 1936 that the Dohnavur Fellowship Hospital was finally completed and opened. Its Tamil name, *Parama Suha Salai*, given to it by a patient, means "Place of Heavenly Healing." That is what it has become during the last fifty years.

So the healings continued, prayer reinforcing medical skill, and many miracles have been seen both in the bodies and souls of patients from that day to this.

Amma rejoiced in this, and she wrote in one of her letters about the greater miracle of spiritual victory in a patient called "Lover of God":

"Lover of God"

She has a TB spine. Her bones are like chalk. She was in our hospital for months, but nothing could give her new bones. Yet, disappointed as she was, she turned to the Lord Jesus in faith and became His true lover.

Her return home led at once into conflict. Not only on special days but often on ordinary days food that had been put before the gods was given to her.

"As I was the Lord's, I could not eat it," she said simply.

This offended her stepmother. Her words were angry.

"Why don't you eat what is put before the gods? You used to do so. Why don't you do so now?"

What could the little Lover answer but that then she had not known her Lord, but now she knew Him and served Him.

"I cannot do this thing."

Then another would come and taunt her. "Well, you have been to Dohnavur and learned about their God. You say He is a living God, and yet He cannot heal you!"

She would reply, "It does not matter if my body is not healed, for my heart is healed. It is in peace. When I die my body will be cremated, but my soul will go to Him in heaven. So healed or not, I trust Him."

Even if one were well and strong and could escape occasionally from the pitiless nagging, it would be difficult. What must it be for one who was never well and strong and could not possibly escape? "My daily furnace is the tongue of man," said St. Augustine, and he at least sometimes could walk out of the furnace. Poor little "Lover of God" had to sit still in the midst of it.

❖ In the tragedy of Vijeya too, Amma saw the miracle of spiritual victory.

Spiritual Illumination

Some of you know a little of what Indian mothers often have to suffer from ignorant handling. Poor Vijeya had been terribly injured. Her people had not been concerned about her suffering. They had put her in an outhouse and left her. When at last they brought her to the hospital, she was in such a state that three operations were required. The last one was very complicated and difficult.

❖ Whenever there is an emergency in the hospital or a difficult operation, a hymn tune is played on the tubular bells in the tower above the operating room. The sound carries to every compound, and all, from oldest to youngest, stop what they are doing and pray for the medical staff and for the patient. The whole family prayed for Vijeya during her third operation.

For some days it was touch and go as to whether the operation had been successful. When on the twentieth day all was well, there was great rejoicing.

Then suddenly the delicate work done in the third operation broke down, and Vijeya was almost where she had been before. She had come to know the Lord, and that evening she wept and said, "I do love the Lord and He has given me His peace, but couldn't you leave me without food for three weeks, and let me go to Him?"

She did not know how to face going on living. But she was led into comfort and willingness for even this. And now her face is radiant.

Surely such a transformation is not of earth. More wonderful than even the most wonderful operation is the miracle of spiritual illumination!

Now what is left to ask and receive for Vijeya? Just this: that the miracle of miracles, which Paul calls being made "more than a conqueror" (Rom. 8:37), may be wrought and maintained in her.

Who can rise to such a prayer? Whoever does so will find that prayer extremely searching, even piercing. Am I, who ask this for one so lately enlightened, living this life myself? Do I turn my sorrows, my most bitter disappointments, "into occasions of gain"? Do I in these things, all of them, more than conquer through Him who loves me?

❖   In her own long life Amma experienced both healing given and healing withheld. In 1931, while inspecting a house in a village where work was commencing, she slipped in the dusk into a pit "dug where no pit should have been." Everyone expected her broken leg and dislocated ankle would soon be mended and she would be back among them as usual. But it was not to be. One illness succeeded another, and for the remaining twenty years of her life, Amma was increasingly confined first to her room, then to her bed.

A year after the fall, she wrote to her family:

Receiving and Reflecting

"But we all, with open face beholding as in a glass [receiving and reflecting] the glory of the Lord, are changed into the same image from glory to glory, even as by the Spirit of the Lord" (2 Cor. 3:18).

I was thinking rather sadly of these long months and of how little receiving and reflecting there has been; then I looked at the photo of moonlit water in my Bible and marveled afresh at its clear beauty, and longed to be a little less unlike that water.

Then I asked Him who is our Sun, our Moon, our Stars, our All, to let me know what hindered this clear reflection. And this came to mind: Years ago I prayed and wrote down and dated the prayer, that I might serve to the last day and then go straight to heaven, never giving work to anyone by being ill.

Again and again, when all but on the verge of a breakdown, strength to carry on had been given, and I believed that I had the petition that I had desired of Him. But now?

Then it was shown to me that the least little whisper of disappointment was like the thin and wandering mist that sometimes rises from a surface of water; where that mist is there can be no perfect receiving and reflecting.

But the very last word that came to me was twice repeated, as it is in John 14:1–27—such a word of love. "Let not your heart be troubled. Let not your heart be troubled."

❖   It was not her own pain and illness that most troubled Amma, but her inability to serve. Two years later she wrote:

God Himself

I had been trying to pull my mind around to what seems to be true—that I should not be able to do all I hoped I would—when I opened my Bible at Deuteronomy 31:2–3: "I can no longer go out and come in. . . . The Lord your God himself will cross over before you."

Can you imagine the comfort it was? It does not much matter that I can no more do all I long to do, if the Lord our God goes before you all, morning by morning into the unknown land of each new day's life, leading and guarding, blessing and loving.

❖   Amma continued to expect healing. Every morning she woke with new hope, only to be disappointed. Years later she wrote:

The Touch

We still look for the Touch to renew strength as it has so often done before. In the meantime I think of the words of a peaceful letter: "Yes, at first I thought healing would come as it had before. Then I saw there was something more blessed than mere healing—to be in the center of His will. Then came His word, 'These all died in faith, *not* having received the promises' (Heb. 11:13), and that settled it for me once and for all. So either way, it will be right. All the paths of the Lord are mercy and truth."

All the paths, not some of them but all. And mercy, I find, means in this verse lovingkindness: "All the paths of the Lord are lovingkindness" (Ps.25:10, RV).

Pray that wherever they may lead, I may *sing* in the paths of the Lord.

But the prayer I most want you to pray for me is Jeremy Taylor's "Take from me all slothfulness, that I may fill up all the spaces of my time." Better still, ask *Him* to fill the spaces day by day for me.

❖   Amma's eyes were always on her Lord. It was His example, His teaching which she longed to follow. There were often times when she was tempted to give in to the sin she nicknamed *Agag*, "that most despicable of sins, self-pity." One night when she could not sleep for pain, she wrote this prayer:

Agag—Self-pity

Not for Thyself, Thy pity and Thy fears,
Not for Thyself, Thy sympathy, Thy tears—
Only for others were Thy comforts spent;
Only for others Thy compassions lent.
        This secret virtue, self-forgetfulness,
        This generous power to succor and to bless
        By reason of an inward liberty,
        Give it to me, my Lord, give it to me!

Now, by Thy grace, I do contemn, refuse
That deadly vice, self-pity. I would use
Strength that Thou givest, pity's gracious power
For others only. Grant me from this hour

To be aware of Agag, though he be,
Like Agag, walking very delicately.
Help me to rise and smite him down and slay,
And spare him not. Away with him—away!

❖ Amma's letters and notes often share with the ill words which helped her during her own long illness.

In the Night

The Prayer Book version of Psalm 17:3 is "Thou hast proved and visited me in the night season. Thou hast tried me and found no wickedness in me; for I am utterly purposed that my mouth shall not offend."

We know the words that our dear Lord spoke in His night season, the night in which He was betrayed; there was no flaw there. Only the Perfect One who speaks in so many of the psalms could use these words as they stand.

But there is hope for us all in another translation (Rotherham's) which has "Thou hast tested my heart, hast made inspection by night, hast refined me until thou could'st find nothing."

Those who find themselves caught in some night of trial or temptation or anxiety, and those of us who are kept awake in the midst of literal night when we long for relief and sleep—to us all these words come with mighty force of eternal encouragement.

It is so easy to slip in patience, to forget that we have utterly purposed that our mouth shall not offend, and find ourselves saying of perplexing circumstances, "Will they never clear up?" Or of a hard soul that nothing seems to move, "Will it never respond?" Or of some anxiety, or even of only a pain that wearies us, "Will it never go away?"

The longer the night, whatever form that night may take, the harder humanly speaking, not the easier, is it to "let patience have her perfect work" (James 1:4), if by patience we mean the valiant patience of hope. So here is a golden word for everyone tried in any such way. The "Father of spirits" (Heb. 12:9) will not cease until He has perfected that which concerns us (Ps. 138:8). He will refine us until He can find nothing.

How can we ever be glad enough that He has told us so? Which of us does not delight in the marginal rendering of Luke 6:40, "Everyone shall be perfected as his Master"? To the Lord, the Doer, be praise forever and ever.

For the Ill

Some know what it is to pray for health and put their will into all that is done to help them get well, and yet they are not well.

Leave that for the moment; think instead of the love, divine love and human too, which has helped you so much. Think of the pain-easing "means" which are from our Father, and of all the happiness He gives in spite of the trial of continued weariness, and the disappointment when you turned a corner which you hoped would lead out into the good open air and it didn't, but doubled back and left you just where you were before— only tireder. Push depressing thoughts away, and let the waves of the love of your Lord wash over you and rest you.

Four hundred years ago Jeanne de Chantal wrote, "We cannot measure the love He showers on souls who give and abandon themselves to Him, and who have no higher aspiration than to do all that they believe to be pleasing to Him."

Let us set our seal to this, for it is true.

Not "What" but "How"

"Strengthened with all might according to His glorious power, for all patience and longsuffering with joy" (Col. 1:11, NKJV).

"That you may know what is the exceeding greatness of His power towards us who believe, according to the working of His mighty power which He worked in Christ when He raised Him from the dead and seated Him at His right hand in the heavenly places" (Eph. 1:18–20, NKJV).

These are tremendous words. I have been letting them soak into me as I pondered the might of His glory on the scale of His majestic resources, "which can amply pour force into our weakness."

I am more and more assured that it does not matter so much *what* we go through as *how* we go through it.

And the more we are cast upon our God, the more we prove His lovingkindness and the more we have to offer Him. "Out of the spoil won in battles did they dedicate to repair the house of the Lord" (1 Chron. 26:27).

Through

"We went through fire and through water, *but* thou broughtest us out into a wealthy place" (Ps. 66:12).

I like that word *through*. Through fire, through water, through the valley of Baca (weeping), through the valley of the shadow of death—we don't *stay* in any of these places. Circumstances may lead us *in*, but God leads us *out* into a wealthy place. We are positively enriched by the fire and the flood. How that must annoy the devil!

Isn't it good that fire and flood are part of a passing phase? "The outside of the [oyster] shell wears away in time, until the inside becomes the outside. But as the outside wears away, the oyster keeps building up the mother-of-pearl inside."

This is a perfect illustration of 2 Corinthians 4:16–18: "Therefore we do not lose heart. Even though our outward man is perishing, yet the inward man is being renewed day by day. For our light affliction, which is but for a moment, is working for us a far more exceeding and eternal weight of glory, while we do not look at the things which are seen, but at the things which are not seen. For the things which are seen are temporary, but the things which are not seen are eternal" (NKJV).

Basket

7

Witness, Conflict and Victory

❖ The passion for souls grew no less even when Amma herself was no longer able to go out to the villages. Instead it grew deeper and stronger. She longed for her family, one and all, to be evangelists, soul-winners. Often she wrote notes to encourage and guide them. She was always eager to hear of individuals they were teaching, in the hospital or in the villages, and she prayed for them faithfully. Many inquirers and converts were brought to her room to see her and pray with her—an experience they seldom forgot.

Long before it was anything but a vision for the future, Amma had thought of a hospital as the main avenue of service and evangelism for her family. Her hopes were realized.

The Hospital

I have always believed that the hospital, with its varied service, is in the thought of our Lord our chief mission field. There are different kinds of work: washing and ironing the hundreds of surgery gowns, towels, dressings and bandages; cooking; scrubbing floors; dispensing; nursing; taking training classes and so on. But there are no distinctions in the work as between secular and spiritual. Everything is done for the furtherance of the gospel.

A hospital can be dead, of course, just as any other work can be dead as to spiritual purposes. But if it be alive, its workers alert and loving and faithful, then it is a rich quarry and whoso digs, finds jewels.

People come from villages out of reach of any itinerating band. They come from hidden-away houses into which no alien could penetrate. They come, and you meet on common ground. You are not forcing yourself upon them as you are when you invade their villages and especially their more private streets. You are not intruding. India hates intrusion.

As the hospital is planned for families, they come in families. Whole households can be taught, and as they are far away from their own people and so not afraid to listen, they can be taught as they could not be at home. The people buy Gospels and Bibles too, and read them unafraid. So the light is spreading.

Pray, for nothing can surpass the ingenuity of the Adversary in devising ways to reduce it to being merely a hospital, not an aggressive force against him and his kingdom. And always the assault comes in some unexpected form.

For all who work there, ask that in the inward life, as well as in the outward, there may be a continual going forth "to all meeting of His wishes, so as not only to obey explicit precepts, but as it were to anticipate His 'sweet beloved will' always, everywhere." (Moule, *Colossian Studies* 1:10)

> Satan trembles when he sees
> The weakest saint upon his knees

We want him to be a trembling not a triumphant devil.

Teaching

The teaching of the many inquirers and converts is a work which goes on steadily all the time. Most of our work is reading and prayer alone with one or another who is turning towards our Lord. Once there is a rooted faith, class work is possible, but much has to be done first. There are stones to clear out of the field before the seed has much chance, and this takes time. You cannot shovel stones away by some patent clearing-up machine. You have to pick them out one by one.

Our idea is not to nurse people and make them weaklings, but to lead them to the strong Savior and then teach them to observe the things He wishes them to do. This takes time, especially with simple minds.

Sowing

"Fear not to sow because of the birds." Mr. Mordant, tutor to the Crown Prince of Siam, hung those words on the wall of his room at the Palace at Bangkok. I want to hang those wise words on the wall of the mind of all God's sowers. The birds of the air are everywhere. What use then to sow? *Fear not to sow because of the birds.*

So often we sow upon the rocky ground, and among thorns, and by the wayside, and waste the good seed. More and more I want to be so led of the Spirit that I shall sow beside all *waters* (Isaiah 32:20), knowing God's mind about people so that I shall feel by a spiritual instinct what part of the great message they need.

"*Rightly dividing* the word of truth" (2 Tim. 2:15)—we often make mistakes there, pressing people to accept Jesus before they have really been convicted and awakened to feel their need of a Savior; or pressing them on to blessings they are not ready for (the fullness of the Spirit, for example) before they know about cleansing and consecration.

To go back to the sowing picture, it is as if we tried to sow before the ground has been broken up by the plowshare, and weeded and watered. There is such a longing to *get on*, always, in our hearts!

Pray that God by His Holy Spirit's power may even now visit the bit of the field He means to send us to. Pray and pray for prepared ground.

"You water its ridges abundantly, You settle its furrows; You make it soft with showers, You bless its growth" (Ps. 65:10, NKJV).

I believe what we call "delays" and "hold-ups" are meant to be used for divine preparation of the ground. Seed sown on rock or sunbaked clay does not usually take root, and much of our ground is naturally just rock and clay as hard as rock. We are never told to sow upon a rock.

There must be something done in a soul before it is ready to listen. We need to learn how to use delays and disappointments for the kind of prayer that calls the showers of God to visit the earth.

There is much teaching for the Lord's husbandman in the last five verses of the Sixty-fifth Psalm.

No Stagnation

Where the Lord is, there stagnation is not. But there are times, even where He is manifestly present, when nothing seems to be doing. It may be that just then the greatest activities are stirring out of sight. What of the time the seed lies under the ground?

What really matters is to make sure that seed of the eternal sort is being sown. Then as a matter of course life will follow life with its ever-wonderful changes and goings-on. No, there is no stagnation with the Lord, the Giver of life.

Soul-winning

Looking back, as I often do now, I cannot help noticing the quietness of God's working. He seems to work in souls as He does in seeds: slowly, imperceptibly but powerfully. No amount of urging makes anyone evangelistically-minded; the longing to win men and women and children for Christ is born from above.

Ask that we may not get discouraged. Discouragement cuts the nerve of love and effort. Satan wants to make us think souls can't be won—or at any rate that they *won't* be—anything to make us give up trying to win them.

Pray that we may not lose heart. The battle is the Lord's! His is the kingdom and the power and the glory—however things look now.

Fireflies

We have very lovely glowworms and fireflies. In the still dark night they shine in the hedges and flit away like living lamps to the darker regions beyond. So clear is their fairy light that by one, I can see to read.

They say so much to me, these silent shining things. Oh to be His glowworms, hidden where only He sees us in some quiet hedge of His planting, lighting it up for Him! May we be His fireflies too, carrying His love-light over the hedge if He beckons so—faraway, where "He goes before."

Let us ask that the stillness in which only His lights can shine may be ever around us, the stillness of the calm of His presence. And oh, let us ask that in this dark world we may so shine that others may see to read His love in the face of our loving Jesus.

Whole-time Service

"Whole-time service"—the phrase has become common of late. But when was a Christian's work not whole-time service? Weaving or preaching (to mention no other way of using his days and nights), was not St. Paul always in whole-time service?

Many have forgotten that unofficial witness-bearing used to be the chief way by which the good news went around the world. I tell you, and you believe and receive and tell somebody else, and he tells others.

Frank, vital telling in ordinary language that the Lord Jesus Christ lives and loves, and can save and keep, and can be known like a real friend, and is a Master who gives real orders and strength to carry them out—think of the power that is in that! Can you wonder that the devil detests it?

Work and Witness

One day an old man said something like this: "We are tired of people who come around talking. Most of them get their food by talking. That is easy work. Why don't you show us the life of your Lord Jesus?"

He meant, "Why don't you live lives such as we have to live—working lives—and show us Christ's life in that way?"

Paul wrote to the people whom he called his crown of rejoicing, "We urge you . . . to work with your own hands, as we commanded you, that you may walk properly towards those who are outside" (1 Thess. 4:11–12, NKJV). And he reminded his dear friends of Ephesus, as he said goodbye to them, how he had lived among them:

> You yourselves know that these hands have provided for my necessities, and for those who were with me. I have shown you in every way, by laboring like this, that you must support the weak. And remember the words of the Lord Jesus, that he said, "It is more blessed to give than to receive." (Acts 20:34–35, NKJV)

One who does honest work and takes every opportunity life gives him to witness to his Lord and to win souls for Him, is surely following in the steps not only of His great servant Paul but of our Lord Himself. For "He went about doing good" —not speaking only, but doing (Acts 10:38).

❖ Amma followed this principle in the upbringing and training of her own children. They have spread out now to many parts of India in many different professions and occupations. A few are in other lands: England, Canada, America, Zambia, Saudi Arabia, Yemen. Wherever they are they remain part of the Dohnavur family, and most of them keep in close touch with home. Amma's prayer that they might be witnesses to the Lord has been answered in the lives of many, but not all, of the scattered hundreds.

Vocation

There is much prayer about the vocation of the boys and girls as they grow up. I have often been struck by the way Paul takes it for granted that men and women to whom he writes would witness for their Lord in their ordinary calling. I cannot find a single appeal to them to leave it and make preaching their one concern.

I don't of course mean that none are called to leave their fishing-tackle and follow in a different way. Some are, and then the call is tremendous. All other calls, all earthly relationships go down before it; for "the kingdom of heaven cannot be established on natural lines." But surely the greater number are meant to "abide in their calling with God" (see 1 Cor. 7:20). I, for one, rejoice in unofficial, spontaneous Christian witness. I have seen the power such witness has.

He Took a Towel

The work for our children leads out to witness and service among the unreached Hindus and Muslims. I had some twenty years of evangelist work at home and abroad before the word came to me, "He took a towel" (John 13:4), so I think I can fairly compare the opportunities given *before* with those given *after* that word came.

At first it seemed an end to everything that I had believed I was called to do, but now after many years of the towel life (serving and bringing up the children) I can only thank Him who held me in obedience to the heavenly vision when many a time I would have turned from it, but for His hand upon me.

Sometimes friends ask what it is that makes such demands upon us. I think chiefly this: There is what Paul calls *travail* "until Christ be fully formed" in these who are given to us (Gal. 4:19). It is not just that there is work to do and that we have to see it is done properly. It is much more than that. We believe India is meant to evangelize India, so our first care is to help and strengthen our dear children who are our fellow-workers.

Few are at once quite selfless. We like to do what we call "direct missionary work" ourselves. But as we go on with our God, we come to the place where we ask Him to take and bless and *break* and give. After that it does not matter what our part in any service be, if only souls are won and His name glorified.

Spiritual Nurture

Remember all who are doing the work of spiritual nurture. Men and women inside and outside our walls, and many boys and girls need patient, faithful Bible teaching.

Such intensive teaching is no luxury. It is all done with a single consuming purpose: "the equipment for work of service" (Moule's *Ephesian Studies*). I don't think we can improve on the first great missionary's way of thinking. He seems to have taken it for granted that the men and women he won for the Lord would evangelize their communities by using the opportunities that came in the course of daily life and common work.

So that their witness might be effective, he taught them to test by the touchstone of His will what is pleasing to the Lord. "How can I please You in this thing and in that? How can my thought meet Yours, and my will have the joy of being laid along the line of Your good pleasure?"

Such teaching takes time. It cannot be hurried. Backed by prayer, it is effectual to the perfecting of souls inside the kingdom and the salvation of souls from without.

The Background

What lies behind the work of soul-winning? Quiet routine work, much prayer, a thousand thoughts worked out into patient deeds, the laying down of private choices. I see each evangelist-hearted teacher as a corn of wheat which has fallen into the ground and died. "If it dies, it produces much grain" (John 12:24, NKJV).

But Bishop Frank Houghton, in *China Calling*, speaks truth when he says the teacher must beware of "neglecting the opportunities of personal witness which life in a heathen country affords. His teaching will gain freshness if he is doing the work of an evangelist, and it is of little use for him to lay upon his hearers the responsibility of witness if he is not himself consumed with a passion for making Christ known to others."

So I delight in knowing that all teachers, and other workers who are able, go out to the villages. Fire kindles fire.

❖ It is not only those working in the hospital who are evangelists. Those who make a home for the children and those who teach in the schools, as well as those who contribute to the well-being of all by their work in the sewing rooms, workshops, kitchens, laundries and gardens, often give their spare time to evangelistic work in the villages. They go out two by two, visiting in homes and, wherever possible, taking meetings for children in the schools. When they return, they have firsthand news for the children which helps them to understand and to pray for those outside their own big family who need Christ so desperately.

Conflict

There is no such thing as spiritual blessing without corresponding fierceness of attack. No conversion, no conflict. Even one conversion, and certain conflict. This is the law of the battle.

There can be no such thing as ultimate defeat, but there

can be very tremendous attack on us as a fellowship. This may take most unexpected forms.

But Isaiah 41:10 says, "Look not around thee" (RV margin). Another rendering is "Look not at thyself." Instead look at God.

> Lord God Omnipotent, King of the Ages,
>   Mighty the waves, like the waves of the sea,
> Flood after flood lifts his billows and rages.
>   What is the noise of those waters to Thee?
>
> Father, we rest in Thee; O let us never
>   Dream of defeat, for defeat cannot be.
> Comfort and strengthen the brave, wheresoever
>   They toil and suffer that souls may be free.
>
> Spirit of Discipline, hold our wills steady,
>   Faithful and peaceful through pleasure or pain;
> Weld us together in comradeship, ready
>   For the great Day of Thy coming again.

❖ It is not only Dohnavur that is attacked; everyone who openly confesses Christ faces tremendous opposition. Yet, though she knew they would suffer terribly, Amma never accepted "secret discipleship." She wrote:

Secret Discipleship

Our experience goes to prove that if the "secret" is kept secret too long it gradually ceases to exist. There is nothing to be kept secret. True faith, even the weakest, seems to flourish better in the open fresh air of confession than in the closeness of secrecy.

❖ But she never underestimated the cost, or ceased to suffer with those to whom it was given not only to believe in Christ, but also to suffer for His sake (Philippians 1:29).

Converts

S— is the third to be converted, so the village is furious. He has lands planted with bananas, and his enemies cut down a thousand plants in a single night—a year's growth just going into fruit. Then they filled his well with cactus.

"If only it were death," he said, "it would soon be over; but this is like smashing the vessel from which I drink."

He has had to sell his land and his well at less than half their value, because it is useless to keep them. The same thing would happen again—and anyway, he has no money for replanting.

What would you do if it cost you so much to confess Christ openly?

Unoffended

For some the piercing experience of John the Baptist is appointed. The son of such a one has just been with us, on his way to see his father who has been for eight months in prison on a false charge. He is called to glorify the Lord "by honor and *dishonor*" (2 Cor. 6:8).

"We will not be offended in Him," he wrote to his wife. In a later letter he writes of those who have shattered his life, "I can pray now, Father, forgive them, for they know not what they do."

Sorrow is either very contracting, causing us to be selfishly absorbed in our own grief, or else it is very enlarging, opening the heart to the griefs of others. This last is clearly our God's intention: "Thou hast enlarged me when I was in distress" (Ps. 4:1).

When the suffering is caused by the devil's wiles, Philippians 1:28 is an exceedingly important word: "And not in any way terrified by your adversaries" (NKJV). *God* has not given us the spirit of fear (2 Tim. 1:7). Then, if it comes, who gives it?

❖   There was not only conflict and suffering when a soul turned to Christ, there was also a wonderful joy. Amma never forgot the day when she and some others visited an old man who had been imprisoned on a false charge. On a previous visit he had been sunk in despair, but Amma had given him a Tamil New Testament and the family had rallied round in prayer for him. Amma recounted the result:

A Free Prisoner

One day we were able to see him. We hardly recognized him. The look of despair was gone.

"I have read, I have read my book," he said, holding it up, "and I have read of One who had torture far worse than mine. And He is here with me!"

The old man's eyes were alight. He stretched out his hands through the bars and held mine, clasping them in joy. He had had no teacher but the Spirit of God, no comforter but the invisible God. His prospects have not lightened. But he was at rest.

"What shall we then say to these things? If God be for us, who can be against us?" (Rom. 8:31).

Touched to the heart, awed by this evidence of the presence of the Lord's love, we came away, leaving him singing to himself the Tamil lyric beginning, "My Redeemer lives; what lack I? Answer, O my soul!" We had read the last few verses of Romans

8 to him, and they sang through our own souls too. "Who shall separate us from the love of Christ?" Not prison bars indeed.

Matthew 25:36

"I was in prison."
O Breath of heavenly air
Blown by the winds of heaven,
Let come what may,
Our hearts will not despair.
Thou wilt not stay away
From any prison
When friend of Thine is there.

"I was in prison."
So Thou art with them there.
The door that opened to them, unaware
Of Thy great Presence, opened unto Thee,
Whom no man can gainsay.
The warders never knew,
Nor had they eyes to see
Whose feet passed through
The door that day.

Basket

8

The Cross and Commitment

❖ The cross was central to all Amma's thinking. She lived in the light of it. She wrote:

Calvary

If only once for one hour, all we could bear to know of what Calvary meant to Father, Son and Holy Spirit could be flashed upon our hearts, burned deep into them—then our thoughts would become transfused with the fire of a love divine and our lives henceforth would be transfigured. And the heathen would know it.

❖ The story of our Lord's passion never became familiar to her, and it was made almost unbearably real as she taught those who were hearing it for the first time. One such was Arulai, an eleven-year-old girl who later became her beloved fellow-worker.

The Cup

Sometimes when Arulai reads for the first time something new about His love, she is too awed to speak about it for a while but just sits and broods over it. One day we were reading about that last night in the Garden of Gethsemane and His prayer, "Father, if it is your will, remove this cup from me."

"What is the cup?" she asked.

One who was with us said, "The suffering of the cross."

"Oh, no!" she answered quickly. "It could not have been that, for I read that when He was going to be crucified He saw some women crying, and He said, 'Don't cry about me. Cry about yourselves.' I don't think it was the cross He minded so much. That could not have been the cup. What was it?"

I proposed that we should read on and see if any light came, so we read the different accounts of those last days and hours. When we came to the prayer on the cross, "My God! My God! Why have you forsaken me?" she stopped, too horrified to read another word. I only said, "Our sins were upon Jesus. So the holy God—" when she broke in, in great distress,

"So the holy God could not look at Him. He turned away! He left Him all alone! Oh! That was the cup."

It was too much for her and for all of us indeed. How real these things seem when you live through them with someone to whom they are all new. Oh how one wonders that they can ever be other than real! How can we get accustomed to the story of such love?

When Jesus Came

In the St. Martin-in-the-Fields' magazine I found these verses (by G. A. Studdert-Kennedy):

When Jesus came to Golgotha
  They hanged Him on a tree;
They drove great nails through hands and feet
  And made a Calvary.
They crowned Him with a Crown of Thorns,
  Red were His wounds and deep,
For those were crude and cruel days,
  And human flesh was cheap.

When Jesus came to Westminster
  They simply passed Him by,
They did not touch a hair of Him,
  They simply let Him die.
For men had grown more tender,
  And they would not give Him pain—
They only just passed down the street
  And left Him in the rain.

If one who reads this has left Him in the rain, think for a minute. You did not mean to do it. Stop doing it now. You would never have done it for one minute if you had known how dear He is.

❖ Amma recounted what happened one year at the family's special evangelistic meeting on her birthday, December 16:

Conviction

The meeting in the evening broke up, as usual, into several groups. In the men's group God worked in power, and the prayer of years was answered. Koruth had them for hours. When he came out he said, "This is the Lord's doing. They have been confessing their sins." A genuine conviction of sin had been granted and a new sense of what Calvary meant.

This is very rare, so rare that some of us cease to expect it. There is plenty of preaching and praying and singing about it; Good Friday sees crowds in church for hours. There is most efficient machinery, wheels of all sorts and sizes are turning all the year round. But oh, for the vital touch of life, the sense that burns like a live cinder pressed into the flesh! It was for *my* sin He died, *I* crucified my Lord.

❖ People who knew Amma find it difficult to think of any fault in her. Not so Amma herself. She was intensely, agonizingly aware of her own sinfulness and what it had cost her Lord to redeem her. She said once that her favorite verse in all the Bible, the verse she could not do without, was 1 John 1:7: "The blood of Jesus Christ his Son cleanses us from all sin." Her prayer for herself and for others was, "From coldness to Thy death and passion, good Lord, deliver us."

She did not believe there could be true, sacrificial service unless there had first been that burning conviction of sin, and of what it meant to a holy God and to our Lord Jesus Himself. "It is at the cross, and only there, that we learn to give," she wrote.

The cross in the life of a Christian meant, to Amma, a daily living out of Galatians 2:20:

Crucified with Christ

"I have been crucified with Christ." What does this mean in plain words?

There is something you longed to do. It was a good thing. You wanted to do it for the help of others. You prayed and worked, perhaps even suffered for it. Your Lord's answer was,

"No, I have another thought for you." What then?

"I have been crucified with Christ." Your longing desire is laid down to be nailed to the cross. No one can pluck out those nails. You will be tempted to try to do so, but in that way lies wretchedness, disappointment, failure.

If you are in touch with your Lord, you take the old word "I have been crucified with Christ; it is no longer I who live, but Christ lives in me; and the life which I now live in the flesh I live by faith in the Son of God, who loved me and gave Himself for me" (Gal. 2:20, NKJV), and you ask for grace to live that word.

This position is the only one that results in detachment from the things of self and freedom for the things of others. It is the life of the corn of wheat of John 12:24. It is the only life worth living.

Seed-corn

"Separated from all in which it had lived before" (Westcott's note on John 12:24).

> As the seed-corn sheddeth on the threshing floor
> That which once was precious—needed now no more—
> So the nearest, dearest that would hold in thrall
> Let Thy winnowing fingers loosen:
>   Love be Lord of all.
>
> As the seed-corn falleth in the quiet ground;
> As it lieth hidden, with nor stir nor sound—
> So would I, Thy seed-corn, deep in stillness fall,
> That of me there may be nothing:
>   Thou be All in all.
>
> As the seed-corn springeth lowly at Thy feet—
> Spear of green uplifteth, yieldeth ear of wheat—

So in tender mercy, though the seed be small,
Let it bring forth for Thy glory
Who art Lord of all.

❖ Amma considered the cross was the only way to win souls also.

Self-Funeral

How one feels one's impotence! A mouse might as well try to overturn the Great Pyramid as one of us seek to win a single soul.

> But God has chosen the foolish things of the world to put to shame the wise, and God has chosen the weak things of the world to put to shame the things which are mighty; and the base things of the world and the things which are despised God has chosen, and the things which are not, to bring to nothing the things that are, that no flesh should glory in His presence. (1 Cor. 1:27–29, NKJV)

Ah! There we have it! The sentence of death passed upon *the flesh*, the baptism *into death*, the dying which lives again in the much fruit; the "not I, but Christ" life. One begins to enter into it a little deeper as day by day He teaches one the absolute uselessness, *and worse*, of all fleshly energy.

"God sends us to the heathen for two purposes: to do them good, and to find a grave for a good self." May He make our self-funeral the greatest fact in our existence.

Crucify

My mother's Bible has been sent to me, and I find this in her writing on the flyleaf: "Crucify what you cannot consecrate, and consecrate what you need not crucify."

We cannot lead another further up the hill than we are willing to go ourselves, or even point to something which, once seen, we have refused. What we ourselves refuse, we cannot inspire others to desire.

"Then He said to them all, 'If anyone desires to come after Me, let him deny himself, and take up his cross daily, and follow Me'" (Luke 9:23, NKJV).

Suffer . . . Serve

I have been thinking much lately of the connection between the gift of suffering in Philippians 1:29 and the gift of service in Ephesians 3:8: "To you it has been granted on behalf of Christ . . . to suffer for His sake"; "To me who am less than the least . . . this grace was *given*, that I should preach among the Gentiles the unsearchable riches of Christ" (NKJV).

Given to suffer; given to serve. What deep, rich love-gifts suffering and service must be. Oh to know Him and the power of His resurrection and the fellowship of His sufferings more! We are impotent for the highest till we have learned what it is to follow, not only on the roads of Galilee and on the sea, but further. Oh to know our Lord in the deepest fellowship of all! How little I know of that.

> I would have thee follow, know Me
>   Thorn-crowned, nailed upon the Tree.
> Canst thou follow, wilt thou know Me,
>   All the way to Calvary?

Oh to enter into the fellowship of His suffering for a lost world!—that from the darker gift of pain may come the brighter gift of service, a fuller passing on of those unsearchable riches

than could not have been possible had He not called one to go
with Him where He keeps His treasures of darkness (Isa. 45:3).

A Good Friday Song

Two verses from one of our songs were chosen for Good
Friday this year:

> See, beyond that leafy bough,
>   Someone walks the garden now,
> Thorns, not roses, on His brow—
>   Bitter, sharp thorns, not roses.
>
> Bitter thorns? Then it must be
>   Our dear Lord; for who but He
> Wears that crown of infamy,
>   Giving us joy of roses.

As the girls sang it, I seemed to see the Beloved One, thorn-
crowned among the trees, and the thought came, "What if our
suffering may pluck a thorn out of that crown?" I thought of
the thousands of His lovers and warriors who are suffering now.
What if each of them is, in very truth, humbly and reverently
too, plucking a thorn from that crown? How well worthwhile
anything would be if that were so.

Painful Ways

Almost everyone seems to be going through painful ways at
present. But they know their God, and as they and we all go
forward and through these rough waters, and step by step climb
our Matterhorns and Everests, we find ourselves drawing nearer
to the day when we shall see His face and He "shall look us out
of pain" forever and ever.

I think one of the devil's favorite devices is to try to make us dwell on the hardness of things in general, and to make us feel as if they would always go on like this. But they will not. They are shadows that pass.

Christ of Easter

O Christ of Easter, Jesus Christ our Lord,
Forever be Thy Name beloved, adored,
From everlasting the eternal Word—
Alleluia! Alleluia!

Not with the pomp of trumpet, drum and fife,
But with the quiet power of endless life,
Conqueror of conquerors, in that awful strife
Thou didst triumph—Alleluia!

Ancient of days, King of eternity,
Who broughtest light and immortality,
Where Thou art, there shall Thy servants be,
And shall serve Thee—Alleluia!

To Thee be glory and dominion,
To Thee, the Father's well-beloved Son,
To Thee, the Risen and the Coming One.
Alleluia! Alleluia!

COMMITMENT

❖ Amma expected the normal Christian life to be one of total commitment, based on a deep personal relationship with the Lord Jesus Christ. "Yes, Lord" might be taken as her motto, and she was always trying to help her family and co-workers to accept the Lord's will with joy and to enter into ever deeper fellowship with Him.

No difficulties could be allowed to stand in the way of implicit obedience and constant abiding in His presence.

Onward Christian Soldiers

One day there was a hard thing to be done, and one of us didn't want to do it.

"I can't," she said; but she added honestly, "at least, I don't like to!"

Now she was very fond of a certain hymn, "Onward, Christian soldiers, marching as to war," and her friend (Amma, of course!), who did not at all intend to give up doing this little difficult thing, began to sing it softly—only putting it rather differently:

> Onward, Christian soldiers,
>   Sitting on the mats!
> Nice and warm and cozy
>   Like little pussycats.
> Onward, Christian soldiers,
>   Oh how brave are we!
> Don't we do our fighting
>   Very comfortably?

She laughed at first; but soon she almost cried, for she saw not only the absurdity of it but the *wrong* of singing one thing and doing another.

So she and her friend knelt down together and asked God to make them true to their hymns and true to their prayers. And then they sang this chorus:

> From all fear of what men think or say,
>   Victory for me! Victory for me!
> From ever fearing to speak, sing or pray,
>   Victory for me! Victory for me!

Lord, in Thy love and Thy power make me strong,
That all may know that to Thee I belong,
And when I'm tempted let this be my song,
Victory for me! Victory for me!

❖ Everyone who visited Amma became aware of an unseen
and very loving Presence with her, for everything around her
was hallowed by prayer, not for herself but for others. God
was the very atmosphere in which she lived. She mentioned
once her constant practice:

I don't think I often read a book or touch a thing given by a
friend without thinking of that friend (known or unknown)
and sending a blessing via heaven.

The Practice of the Presence

Long ago when I taught our little ones, I found that they
always wanted me to enjoy everything with them. They would
look up after a few intent minutes over their beads or their
plasticine and say, "Look, Amma! Amma, look!" There was the
constant communion of love and interest and pleasure between
us, a sharing of everything.

The little child in the kindergarten is never unaware of the
presence of her teacher. We are not meant to be unaware of the
presence of the One who loves us most of all, to whom all our
doings matter.

This is the practice of the presence of God.

❖ In her book *His Thoughts Said . . . His Father Said*, Amma
wrote down many of the conversations she had with her heavenly Father when she brought Him her puzzles and her temptations, her doubts and her fears. There were many more such

conversations, and one that she recounted to her family was based on Proverbs 25:4: "Take away the dross from the silver, and there cometh forth a vessel for the finer [the silversmith]" (AV and RV):

He Wants Us

Think of it. Think all round it. Think of the rough bit of oneself. "That's all I am in myself," despairingly I tell Him.

But He says, "I will turn my hand upon thee, and thoroughly purge away thy dross, and will take away all thy alloy" (Isa. 1:25, RV).

"But Lord, You will tire of me long before I am half refined."

"He shall *sit* as a refiner and purifier of silver, and he shall purify and purge as gold and silver" (Mal. 3:3).

He shall *sit*, sit with the long patience of the silversmith of the East, sit unhurriedly, unweariedly.

"O Lord, it is too good to be true, had You not said it. But one thing more may I ask You? Is it possible You are not tired of me yet?"

Straight back comes the answer, "A vessel *for* the silversmith."

So little is He weary of us that He wants to have us altogether and forever for Himself. He *wants* us. Oh, the joy of being His wanted one!

Shall He not have His own way with us? He knows what He is refining us for—we don't. We know *who* it is for, though, and that is quite enough. Let Him take away the dross from the silver, and there shall come forth a vessel for His honor, for His use.

Let us give His love full scope. Nothing happens by itself, and every sorrow, every trial, is part of the plan of love, part of the refining.

Love meant it.

Love sent it.

Love will bless it.

"Is it not lawful for me to do what I will with mine own?" (Matt. 20:15).

Basket

9

Walk in the Spirit

❖ Amma lived in constant fellowship with her Lord. She obeyed the command of Hebrews 3:1 and also verse 13: "Fix your thoughts on Jesus" (NIV) . . . Exhort one another daily." Almost every day, for about eighteen years, she shared with her beloved family the thoughts and insights the Lord gave her, encouraging them to "walk in the Spirit."

There was a wooden plaque hanging on a wall of her room (where she could see it from her bed) with the words, "By one that loveth is another kindled." Amma's own love for the Lord was a consuming passion, deep and intimate, and she longed for everyone else to love Him too.

LOVE

A Great Longing

A great longing comes to me that every heart should offer tenderest love and adoration to our Lord today. Oh that His love may be satisfied by our love! Love does so earnestly desire love that nothing else can satisfy it. It is very wonderful that He should so desire our love, but we know that it is true.

"Your love is better than wine," we say to Him, and His delight is to say to us, "How much better than wine is *your* love" (Song of Sol. 1:2, 4:10, NKJV).

Two verses have shown to me two pictures. "I have set you to be a light to the Gentiles, that you should be for salvation to the ends of the earth" (Acts 13:47, NKJV) and "Who for the joy that was set before him endured the cross" (Heb. 12:2). The joy was that utterly unselfish joy of being a light to us and salvation to us. He loved me and gave Himself for me (Gal. 2:20).

We love You, Lord Jesus, our Beloved; we love You and give ourselves to you.

❖ Amma's confidence in the love of God was not due to blindness to the sin and suffering in the world. She read widely, and of her as of Paul it could be said, "Who is made to stumble and I do not burn with indignation?" (2 Cor. 11:29, NKJV). She pondered long and deeply over "the dark enigma of permitted wrong."

The Dark Enigma

I often think of the first question one of our naughtiest small girls asked, "Why doesn't God *stamp* on that bad Satan?" I could only say, "I don't know."

"The dark enigma of permitted wrong" is with us still. The answer theologians give to that child's question has never satisfied me. I think that the truest and most satisfying answer is, "The secret things belong to the Lord" (Deut. 29:29).

There are times when the things that happen in the world run so cruelly contrariwise that with one voice they appear to deny the existence of Ordering Love. Not God but the devil reigns, so they affirm; and they shout in scorn, "God sovereign? If so, why this?"

But sometimes, and suddenly, He who stands within the shadows moves forth, and the very things that shouted those loud questions are turned to witness to the truth that verily He reigns.

The Judge

The mystery of why young children are not delivered from evil is one I dare not dwell upon. I can only trust that whatever they may become, *God sees them as they would have been had they had the opportunity to be good.* I must believe this, otherwise where is justice? And we know that our God is just.

I am so glad that it is the God of infinite understanding who will judge. It is such rest to remember He knows all, and loves and pities too.

❖ Amma saw God do great miracles, supply tremendous needs, show forth mighty power; but it was the little intimate touches of His love which meant most to her.

Small Things

It is very little things that draw the heart out in tender love to Him who is so near to us, and so loving in His thought for us that nothing is too small for Him to notice or to do. "I will sing unto the Lord, because he hath dealt so lovingly with me" (Ps. 13:6, BCP).

I read that Sir James Jeans said there must be more stars in the sky than there are blades of grass upon the earth. And yet each star is called by its own name (Ps. 147:4).

Have we ever fathomed our Savior's words, "The very hairs of your head are all numbered"? (Matt. 10:30). If anything in human life is too small for His regard, then God is not the God of revelation.

But the God and Father of our Lord Jesus Christ is in very truth our Father and our God. "I ascend unto my Father and your Father, to my God and your God" (John 20:17) is a word upon which faith can hang whatever the new discoveries of science be.

After all, they may dazzle us with their awful greatness, but they take us first into infinitesimal minuteness of structure, "to the region of atoms and molecules which have dimensions in the various directions of the order of a hundred millionth of an inch" (*Concerning the Nature of Things* by William Bragg).

And we find God there, our Father and our God. And more, "This is my Beloved and this is my Friend, O daughters of Jerusalem" (Song of Sol. 5:16).

❖ Often Amma was unable to sleep, and one night she was lying awake thinking and praying about some of the needs and problems of the work.

Suddenly a verse of Scripture flashed into her mind. Next morning she wrote:

Nothing Too Small

"Behold, I am the Lord, the God of all flesh: is there anything too small for me?"

Do you know what it is to hear a text misquoted? It is like a wrong note in music. Instinctively I corrected it, "Is there anything too *hard* for me?" The answer of course was, "Ah, Lord God! Behold, you have made the heavens and the earth by your great power and outstretched arm. There is nothing too hard for you" (Jer. 32:17).

But it persisted the other way: "Is there anything too *small* for me?" till I answered—who could have helped it?—"Ah, Lord God! *There is nothing too small for you.*"

Will you try it the next time your thoughts keep you awake at night?

❖ Amma never forgot our Lord's words in John 15:12: "This is My commandment, that you love one another as I have loved you" (NKJV). That was the standard He set, a standard she dared not lower. Many of her notes to her family and co-workers repeat and underline and illustrate this command, for it was vital if the fellowship was to be truly one in the Lord.

True Love

We are called to the life of truth in love and love in truth. "Speaking the truth in love" (Eph. 4:15). "Let love be without hypocrisy" (Rom. 12:9, RV).

Often the truth is spoken but not kindly, and that leads to trouble. Or a kind heart is tempted to palliate truth for fear of hurting or for fear of losing affection; and that leads to weakness. St. Augustine's prayer must be ours:

> To my fellow-men a heart of love.
> To my God a heart of flame.
> To myself a heart of steel.

God forgive us if we lower our Lord's standard to the usual flabby thing that passes so often for love. We can love too little—never, never too much.

It is worthwhile to study what our Lord meant by love. His life shows it. Courage to hold a beloved soul to the highest;

patience with weakness; hope and a glorious overlooking of falls when He saw true love behind; infinite tenderness—a study of His life will show all this and more.

❖ One year at the meeting on Amma's birthday, the family watched while a chunk of stone containing uncut opal was passed through fire. Later Amma wrote:

The Opal

On the table beside me is the rough opal which went through the fire. Its colors are much more beautiful since then.

The love of the Father never holds a beloved one back from the fire, if by going through it His eternal purposes of blessing can be fulfilled.

"And I have declared to them Your name, and will declare it, that the love with which You loved Me may be in them, and I in them" (John 17:26, NKJV). The love with which the Father loved the Son was not a love which spared and sheltered Him. It was a love which gave Him up to death, even the death of the cross.

Few of us ever even desire such love as this. Fewer perhaps have felt it possible to help any other to desire it; and fewer still have fortitude enough to hold a loved one to a life which fulfills this love.

God forgive the easy love of His lovers. Pass us, O Lord, through the fire, that the colors of love may shine forth.

It cannot ever be easy to hold one another to the highest, but His love in us can make it possible. Not to rise to it is to miss that which He so much desired for us that on that last night, the night on which He was betrayed, He spoke of it to His Father. He longed that it should be in us.

Shall we ask for one another that we may not avoid these deeper calls of love, but truly meet His heart's desire at any cost, *at any cost*?

❖ As well as the children, continually women in need of shelter were brought to Dohnavur, where they were welcomed and loved and taught about the Lord. Between thirty and forty women of mixed ages and very mixed backgrounds and castes lived together in the "Place of Confidence," built in 1937.

Many were truly converted, and some stayed on to help with the work in various capacities. Others after a year or two, or even less, moved away. Almost all had tragic stories; often they were deserted wives, and some had been forced into prostitution and wanted to escape.

A few were entirely undisciplined, usually illiterate, often rebellious and quarrelsome—and seldom, after the first relief of finding sanctuary had worn off, grateful. They called for something more than normal human love. Amma wrote:

Broken Things

I had a letter asking me if we really could possibly love these with whom life has dealt so hardly that "broken things" is the only word to describe them. I can only answer such a question by another: Does our Lord Jesus not love them? Has He not room in His heart for them?

But it can be very difficult. They can be very hard. Often things happen that drain human love dry. Nothing but the divine is any use then. God give us Calvary love, love that cannot be tired out of loving; love that never says, "I have borne enough, done enough, suffered enough."

The agony of crucifixion could wring nothing from our Lord's heart of love but the cry, "Father, forgive them." Perhaps one has to reach the very end of one's natural human love before one realizes what ocean depths of love were in that cry.

JOY

❖ Amma always seemed to be happy. No matter how busy or tired she was, no matter how ill and how much pain she was suffering in her later years, she never lost her sense of humor; there was always an infectious joy about her.

"Religion"

Aren't you sorry for the poor people who find "religion," as they call it, dull? I expect, however, I should find it dull if I went in for it. I don't, in their sense of the word at any rate. I can look back on a good many years now, and anything less dull than life has been to me I cannot imagine.

I find Christ a most glorious Leader, always leading on to something better than the last. Nothing I ever saw of life in earlier days, when it lay before me all vivid and glowing, can compare for sheer delight with the days that have been given since everything went down before the compelling power of the Lord Jesus Christ and Him crucified.

This may reach someone who is at the parting of the ways. Do take my word for it; go on to prove your Lord. The entrancing things of a life spent partly for the things of time are just nothing beside those prepared for those who will go all the way with Him.

But let it be all the way. Halfway following leads nowhere.

Joy Is the Grace We Say to God

"O let your songs be of him and praise him, and let your talking be of all his wondrous works. Rejoice in his holy name: let the heart of them rejoice that seek the Lord" (Psalm 105:2–3).

I do delight in these commands that tell us to do just what everything in us makes us want to do. The musical want to make music, so "Sweep the strings to Jehovah," "Make ye music to him," "Play skillfully." The singers want to sing, so "Sing ye to him," "O let your songs be of him." And all His lovers want to tell of the loving things He is continually doing, so "Let your talking be of him."

We see a rose, and our first instinct is to smell it and enjoy its loveliness. Suppose the Maker of the rose became suddenly visible, standing beside the rose bush, and said, "Do smell it and enjoy it." It is like that.

"Go and see what Tommy is doing and say *Don't.*" This is the wrong way to bring up a child. It is not our Father's way. His is much nicer. He makes us want to do happy things and then He says, "Do them." Dullness, restraint, nervousness, fear—these things are simply not in the picture. Psalmist and apostle (and often in the Psalms it is the Lord Jesus speaking) pile up words of joy to show the light and the liberty of the sons of God—the happy God.

This does not cross out discipline or inner sensitiveness, but it is the life of the Christian in flower. Our Bible shows life whole. It is not always dwelling on the root underground (which must be if there is to be this flower in sunshine); it goes on to flower and fruit.

"In your presence is fullness of joy"—there and here. "At your right hand there are pleasures for evermore." Don't let us postpone the joy and the pleasures as if they belonged only to the life further on. They are for today as well as for tomorrow.

So today's word is, "Let the heart of them rejoice that seek the Lord." "Joy is the grace we say to God."

The Happy God

Man is the only animal, as far as I know, who laughs. This power to enjoy a joke, to laugh, to see the funny side of things, makes it possible to carry on without breaking when without it we would crash. So it is not a small thing that we have received, and it must represent a definite thought of love in our Father's heart. It is a sort of extra, like color.

Do we take it for granted, as too many of us take our good things for granted? Or do we look up and say, "Thank You, thank You very much"?

"Blessed are the single-hearted for they shall enjoy much peace"—and much fun too. If we are single-hearted, disentangled from thoughts of ourselves, we shall see a thousand little delights in the common things, even the difficult things, of life. There is no dullness in the lives of those whose one occupation is "the glad message of the glory of the Happy God" (1 Tim. 1:11, Rotherham).

❖ Amma's own irrepressible sense of humor bubbled over in many of the poems she dashed off, sometimes on the spur of the moment, for the enjoyment of her children. Many were turned into action songs, played and sung with great gusto even today. Here is one example:

Do Your Best

Donkey's bray
  Seems to say,
    "Oh to sing a song!"
But though I
  Really try,
    Somehow the tune goes wrong.

"Aiyaiyo!
  Well I know
    I can only bray."
Do your best,
  Leave the rest,
    That's a good donkey's way.

"In the Ark,
  In the dark,
    All the poor things wept.
'Twas my time,
  And my chime
    Up to the high roof swept.

"They looked 'round
  At the sound—
    Shouted, 'Hip Hooray!'
Rubbed their ears,
  Wiped their tears,
    All on a wisp of hay.

"So you see
  If like me
    You are only you,
Do your best,
  Leave the rest;
    That's what you'd better do."

❖ For Amma, joy was not just the happiness one felt when all was going well. It was something deeper; it was a settled attitude of the mind, and it was usually linked with suffering.

Joy and Suffering

There is a joy set before us, there is joy now—the joy of the Lord, which is something quite apart from ordinary happiness. Spiritual prosperity and spiritual joy are always connected with suffering. In Isaiah 53:10–11, suffering beyond our power to understand is described, and then comes, "and the *pleasure* of the Lord shall prosper in his hand."

Of Paul our Lord said, "I will shew him how many things he must suffer for my name's sake" (Acts 9:16). Paul describes some of these things in 2 Corinthians 11:24–28: beatings, stonings, shipwrecks, perils of all kinds, labor and travail, hunger and thirst, cold and nakedness among them. Yet he could say, "Now I rejoice in my sufferings" (Col. 1:24).

The joy of the Holy Spirit is mentioned in connection with suffering: ". . . in much affliction, with joy of the Holy Spirit" (1 Thess. 1:6, NKJV).

See also Psalm 43:4: "Then will I go to the altar of God [the place of sacrifice], to God my exceeding joy; and on the harp will I praise You, O God, my God" (NKJV).

If we don't hold back from the cost, we shall prove it true: "When the burnt offering began, the song of the Lord began also" (2 Chron. 29:27).

A day or two ago I had a special joy. Some who had to do a difficult thing asked for prayer that it might be done with as much joy as if it had been a pleasant thing. This is victory. This is the sort of thing the angels love to see. It must remind them of their Lord and ours who said, "I delight to do Your will, O my God" (Ps. 40:8, NKJV).

When we think of what that will meant to Him, we are utterly ashamed that ever anything seems hard to us. What a nothing our worst suffering is, in comparison with Calvary.

To Be Wondered At

Last night I woke with something that always brings our dear Lord very near, for it is a kind of piercing in the palm and back of the hand, like the nails that pierced Him. I was being kept in a lovely sort of happiness in spite of it, when the word that I had heard myself saying aloud as I woke came again. It was David's, "I have become as a wonder to many, but You are my strong refuge" (Ps. 71:7, NKJV).

I said to our Lord Jesus, "Lord, I am a wonder to myself! Nothing but Your power could give this happiness. It is not of me at all. And I do wonder how You manage to do it!"

Presently these words came, "To be wondered at in all them that believe." I knew that meant the most pure glory to Him, people forgotten, everything forgotten but the wonder of Him —and we shall be among those who wonder, and see the world wonder at our Adorable One. What does anything matter if this day be drawing near?

But the word "wondered at" puzzled me. Was it not "admired" in 2 Thessalonians 1:10? No, "To be wondered at" persisted.

In the morning I looked up the word in *Young's Analytical Concordance*, and there (wasn't this nice?) the meaning "to be wondered at" was given; and various translations, I found, followed this thought.

Is it not a wonder that He bears with us, has such long patience with us, forgives us so freely when we fail Him and disappoint Him (and ourselves too), heartens us to try again, and pours His sweet gift of happiness into us, unworthy as we are? We can only wonder, knowing it is not of us at all. And what will it be when He "comes to be the world's Wonder"? Even so, come, Lord Jesus.

❖ It was hard for the family to do without Amma's happy presence among them. The older ones looked back to "the good old days" and found it difficult to accept the changed conditions. Amma found it hardest of all, but typically her thoughts were not for herself but for her beloved family. She wrote to them:

Rejoice Always

Some are being tempted to look back and wish for what was, instead of rejoicing in what is and in what shall be.

"Rejoice always" (Phil. 4:4): that is what our God wants us to do, and not to do it is to fail. "All His biddings are enablings." This bidding, then, is also an enabling.

I have a clock in my room which has a fairly loud tick. It is saying over and over just one word: com-fort, com-fort. In *Young's Analytical Concordance*—that invaluable book—I find that to console, solace, soothe is less frequently the meaning of the word translated "comfort" in our New Testament than other words which mean "to call (help) alongside, to refresh, brace."

So the word is like great music, reviving, uplifting, and the God of all comfort does far more than soothe us in trouble—though He does that too.

And so we can live in the last verse of our Forest song, for every day is "this Thy day." Psalm 118:24 says, "*This* is the day that the Lord hath made; we will be glad and rejoice in it." And every place where He is with us is "this dear place."

> And not to this dear place belongs
>   Aught but the good and gay.
> Be all my thoughts like wild birds' songs
>   On this Thy day.

PEACE

❖   Outside the door of Amma's room is a wooden board with the words, "The Room of Peace." It is a true description of a room where the Prince of Peace was truly Lord. Amma wrote:

The Net Curtain

A mauve-colored net curtain hangs in front of my bed. Outside, bordering the path down which many people pass, are some fine tamarind trees. On a dull, rainy day I see the net curtain. Every crease shows. But when the sun is shining I hardly see the net, I see only the splendid trees; their beauty, their greenness holds my eyes. So when the sun is shining I cannot see the net (that is still there) for the glory of that light.

The things that are seen are there. They are not taken away. But if only there is the clear shining on the other side, then we see through the temporal to the eternal, and there is peace in that and radiance, and the glory of the Lord.

"You will keep him in perfect peace, whose mind [imagination] is stayed on You" (Isa. 26:3, NKJV). Blessed be God; He knows the torturing power of imagination. It is possible to stay even that most wayward part of oneself on Him and be kept in peace.

❖   Amma tried not to forget the lessons the Lord taught her.
Beside many verses in her Bible she wrote a date and a brief
word, recalling how that verse had helped her. She did not
forget the visions He showed her either, as the following note,
written at a time of uncertainty about the future of the
fellowship's work, shows:

The Nest

What are storms but opportunities to prove God's keeping
and His peace? Let the winds blow; it is still as it was long ago,
when in a dream I saw black clouds flying, chased by a hurri-
cane, and coming out from among the inky clouds a hand. In
the hand was a wild bird's nest and in the nest three blue eggs.

He who has held that nest (the fellowship) in the hollow of
His hand all through the years, holds it there today. The nest is
safe. The three blue eggs are safe. And so are all the nests everywhere, and all nestlings too.

For Busy Days

I have found much rest in times of pressure in a verse I only
noticed lately. The days were very full at the time I came across
it, and they seemed far too short for all that had to be got into
them. I was beginning to feel rushed when in my morning reading this word came: "He is your life and the length of your
days" (Deut. 30:20, NKJV).

I took the last half as literally as the first, and it brought
calm to my heart and the rush went out. When it came back, I
stopped and remembered the day could never be too short for
what He meant me to put into it, if He Himself was its length.
Isn't it nice to think of days measured like that!

Strength for the day; His joy our strength; strength for soul and strength for body; *He Himself* our very life and the length of our days—what is there left to ask for? Just that quietness of spirit that won't get rushed however tumbling-on-top-of-the-other the day's duties seem to be. They can't really be like that; they only seem to be so on specially busy days.

All the strain goes the minute one remembers in whom lies the day's length; a little measured space in which it is possible to be always peaceful in spirit.

PATIENCE

❖ Amma was not naturally patient. Her nickname in the villages was "The Hare Lady," because she was always hurrying, anxious never to waste time.

She was seldom impatient *with* her children, but she was often impatient *about* them, longing for them to be made perfect in a day. She wrote:

Patience

Sometimes I wonder why our Father takes so much trouble to teach His children patience, for we shall not, I suppose, need that virtue in heaven. Perhaps it is because there is something waiting to be done which cannot be done except by those who are "perfect and complete, lacking nothing." So "let patience have its perfect work" (James 1:4, NKJV).

The thing I feel the need of most, just now, is wisdom and spiritual power in dealing with our girls and children. Each has something in her or about her which sends me to God many a time in a sort of desperation of desire to see it put right there and then. I have so little patience naturally, not a scrap of the real thing I'm afraid. Oh, to see Christ formed in them, and oh, to wait with His patience till the forming is complete!

They are not hard, only as yet very imperfectly converted. Why have we any imperfect? Because there is still such a person as the devil in the world. Even in a Christian family of six or seven, though there is the same good background for all, there is often one who gives anxiety. In a family of 800, each with an unknown and often bad background, can we wonder if we have to go through anxious days?

But we have seen so many miracles that I think truly "despairing of no man" is more than a slogan to us (Luke 6:35, RV margin). "*Now you shall see what I will do*" (Exod. 6:1, NKJV). We have seen, and we shall see. What cannot the Spirit of God effect? We have a God who is at home in dealing with dispositions. And what is heredity to the King of eternity?

Golden Delight

We have a tree here called *peltophorum* by the learned, but Golden Delight is my private name for it. I got it in 1916 and watched year by year for flowers. They never came. This year it is covered with spikes of golden flowers ending in little brown balls of buds, and alighting like butterflies on the golden spikes are scores of flashing little sunbirds. All this against the blue of the clear blue sky—can you imagine the delight of it?

Fourteen years, and at last flowers. But they were worth waiting for. Souls are worth waiting for too. But we do long for them not to miss all that their flowering would mean.

Much Patience

Sometimes certain words in our Bible reading shine out as

though they were written in light. Two words have shone like that in my reading of 2 Corinthians 6:2–10 this morning: *much patience.*

Nine things are mentioned that ask for much patience: tribulations, needs, distresses, stripes, imprisonments, tumults, labors, sleeplessness, fastings. It is good sometimes to take each of these words and think of what they really meant to the man who wrote them.

We often think that we need a good deal of patience for our work and life, and it is true that we do. But the more we ponder those nine tremendous words, the less we shall think of anything we are allowed to do or to endure.

And yet even we need "much patience." It helps if we remember that our God, who is the God of patience, is with us and that He has patience enough for us all.

Unto All Patience

"In all power empowered, continuously (the participle is present) according to the might of His glory, to all patience and longsuffering with joy. And then—what is to be the resultant stream? Not primarily a rush of energies, a torrent of witness, a blaze of miracles. It is to be unto all patience" (Moule on Col. 1:11).

God help us to witness and not to refrain from witnessing, that others may be drawn to seek and find the treasure that is for all. But oh, may He give it to us indeed to be strengthened with all might unto all patience and longsuffering with joyfulness, for we have need of patience. The race is not run yet.

FAITH

God Can Do Anything

We have a God who can do anything. It is not He who fails, but we, with our poor expectations and low hopes. God forgive us and lift us up to the measure of His purposes and His promises.

One night lately I woke suddenly with a word ringing through me: Nothing is impossible for the devil to attempt; nothing is impossible for the Lord to achieve; for "Greater is He that is in you than he that is in the world" (1 John 4:4).

In the Revised Version of Romans 4:19–20, we read that Abraham *considered* the tremendous difficulties ahead; he did not shirk them. Young says the word "considered" means to "perceive thoroughly with the mind." He looked at the difficulties, but he looked at the promises too. "Yea, looking unto the promise of God, he wavered not through unbelief, but waxed strong through faith, giving glory to God, and being fully assured that what he had promised he was able also to perform." And our amazing God who quickens the dead and calls the things that are not as though they were (1 Cor. 1:28) did not allow him to be confounded.

Sooner or later God always opens the door of deliverance to a true seeker. Such a one is much more likely to stand than one whose way is smoothed by us. We need to learn to pray and to count on the supernatural where souls are concerned. I have known Him send (as I believe) an angel to guide a girl out of her prison and bring her through a tangle of lanes into the path that led to our house. And then, like the angel who set Peter free and left him after they had passed through the street (Acts 12:10), that angel disappeared and the girl came on in safely, alone.

Test of Faith

I think by far the greatest test of faith is the frustration that is so often allowed. A worker who can fill a gap no one else can attempt to fill is attacked by some wretched germ and disabled for years. "No one is indispensable," says the shallow thinker. Perhaps not, but some are irreplaceable, and they are not replaced. Doesn't God care about that gap on the precipice edge?

One day, when I was pondering this, the answer came in the form of a question. *What if God is preparing us all for something as yet unrevealed?* If we do not know His purpose, we cannot understand the means He takes to effect it.

That is where faith comes in. "I cannot understand," we say. We are trusted not to try to understand.

Psalm 57:1–2, 7 is the word then: "My soul trusts in You; and in the shadow of Your wings I will make my refuge, until these calamities have passed by. I will cry out to God Most High, to God who performs all things for me"—all things for me, all things for those I love better than myself. And so, "My heart is steadfast, O God, my heart is steadfast; I will sing and give praise" (NKJV).

Rock Crystals

I have been given some stones from Switzerland. One of them is full of rock crystals. Looked at in an ordinary way they look ordinary. Looked at in electric light the stone is a little jewel mine. As I turn it I see tiny stars like diamonds sparkling all over it, and the larger crystals are little pillars of wonder. On a single crystal face there is deep purple, kingfisher blue and rose.

Don't you think sometimes our days look like my stone as

it lies on the table, dull and rather ordinary? Isn't it good to know that one day we shall see these very days illuminated? They will shine then. Each little event in them will take color. We shall see our days then as God sees them now, if only, by His daily grace enabling us, we live in the light with no covered sin, no self-choice between us and that pure light of God.

If in the morning you offer your day to the Lord Jesus Christ, then leave the matter in peace, for He will certainly put into the hours as they pass just what He wants to be there.

❖   A verse sent by one of Amma's family summed up her feelings: "I have found such a lovely verse, the French version of Psalm 143:8, 'Let me hear thy voice of love when I awake. Let me know thy will for today, for unto thee have I handed over my life.' It seems the right verse and prayer for every day of the year."

HOPE

Never be surprised at any sin in man. Never be surprised at any kindness of God. Never think anything too much for the surpassing greatness of His might to effect. Never be surprised at any disappointment. But do not sit down under it. Carry on, carry through.

God is not surprised at human sin and failure. I think that we should, much more than we do, take the same line as our Master and refuse to be surprised out of our hope.

Our hope is in God. I think *expectation* is a gift of the Spirit, and the devil does not like us to get it. He dilutes it if he can. The impossible is all around us. Oh for the sort of faith which can look it straight in the face and not waver!

But it can never be a little thing to see His grace rejected; it is hard to hope then. And always there must be the dagger-thrust question when the matter concerns one very near, "Lord, why this defeat? O Lord, *is it I*?"

> O blessed Hope of God
>   Flow through me patiently,
> Until I hope for everyone
>   As Thou hast hoped for me.

Basket

10

Guidance and Goads

❖ Amma was so manifestly guided by God throughout her long life that it is easy to assume she never made mistakes. That was not so; but she always learned from her mistakes, as the following passage, condensed from a long letter describing an early experience in Sri Lanka, shows:

Mistaken Guidance

A missionary asked me to speak at a children's meeting in Colombo. Before I sent any answer, they put my name in the paper as one of the speakers. I wrote then, saying I had not accepted and could not go unless the date fitted the YWCA meeting (at which I was due to speak). I concluded that *if* the dates fitted it would be "circumstances" pointing it out as His will for me.

A letter came saying they had got the YWCA to alter the date of their meeting so as to make things fit. So I wrote saying I would be there.

About two hours after my card had gone, I saw my mistake. First, I should not have planned a circumstance to help me to know His will; and then I should not have accepted *it* as guide when all other guidance was withheld.

There was no way out of it but the way back. Better be thought discourteous than be untrue to Him. He had not told me to go, so go I could not. By the next post a withdrawal went, and I had peace. I don't know what they will think of me, but I can't help it.

True Guidance

We need three things in all true guidance: the Word, the inward voice and the leadings of circumstance. The first two we can't see; the last we can. It *alone*, as in my case in Ceylon (Sri Lanka), can't lead, but it confirms the other two previously given.

So let us see to it that no force of circumstance shall press us into a move about which we have not clearly got the mind of the Lord.

Sometimes God leads us so that even though the third sign (circumstances) is wanting, we *must* go forward. I think in the story of the two water-crossings we have His first and second lessons in guidance. In the first instance (Exodus 14:13) the people might stand still and see. It seems as if the moment before they stepped in, the Red Sea was divided, so that their first step was on dry ground. If so, though they needed faith to go forward and go on, believing that the watery walls would be kept congealed, it was not faith at high tension. It is so much easier to believe *after* we see than before.

When they crossed Jordan (Joshua 3:8, 15) things were different. There was a swollen river, banks uncertain, a rushing torrent which tore along and showed no signs of stopping. But the command was to go right on, to go right in. And it wasn't shutting your eyes and taking a header; it was to be done in the coolest and calmest possible manner. They were to stand still in Jordan.

God doesn't want us to rush. Especially when we are meditating a "leap in the dark," a "venture of faith"—what names for simple obedience!—let us stand still in Jordan. Then comes the triumph, but not till then. Until *after* they obeyed there were no "circumstances" to guide, only His bare word.

We must be sure before we move one inch. To be capable of being made sure, we must be living in everyday nearness. We can't get suddenly into the full beams of the lamp to our feet and the light to our path (Ps. 119:105) if we have been walking for a while in the twilight. As for the eye-guidance of Psalm 32:8, we can only read the eyes of those we know and know well. "I will instruct you and teach you in the way you should go; I will guide you with My eye" (NKJV).

So it all points to our need of care, lest we mistake our own moods for the Spirit's leading. The only possible way to keep out of such perilous ground is to *keep close.*

Oh to know our God so well that all misunderstandings shall be quite impossible! Paul meant a good deal when he said, "That I may know him" (Phil. 3:10).

❖ There were questions about guidance which Amma was often asked. One was, "How can I be sure of my own guidance?"

Three Tests

There are three tests which I have found helpful.
1. Is what appears to me "guidance" in line with the general tenor of Scripture?

2. Have I some word that I can recognize as my Lord's to me?
3. When I am nearest God, is there peace in my heart about it and a quiet sureness?

The Scriptures teach us that personal desires don't count. We follow a crucified Savior, so that anything that has *I* in it cannot be guidance. In community life one cannot act apart from others; each has to consider the other (Gal. 6:2; Phil. 2:4). How will this, that I think of as guidance, affect others?

Test yourself by this question: "If I am mistaken, am I as glad to yield as I would be to go forward?" If not, "This persuasion does not come from Him who calls you" (Gal. 5:8, NKJV).

If the word is His, He will so deal with circumstances that I can obey it. Sometimes the way opens as the Red Sea did before the children of Israel so that they went over dry shod. Sometimes it is as it was later, when the waters of Jordan did not divide till the feet of the priests were dipped in the brim of the water. What is certain is that sooner or later, if He is leading on, He deals with my circumstances so that all is clear.

"If in doubt, do nou't [nothing]" is a Cumberland saying which often helps. If the peace of God does not fill your heart and mind, if there is an up-and-down feeling, a question mark over the matter, don't move.

❖ Another question sometimes asked was, "How can I be sure that the one who is advising me is truly showing me the will of God?" Amma's answer has a message for all engaged in counseling, as well as for those who seek advice:

Counseling

Is your counselor pointing you to the highest and most heavenly, and so perhaps hardest? Or does he lead you towards the easier course? Does he help towards self-ease or self-discipline? Does he change his advice to suit your moods? Does he say soft things lest he should offend you or lose your affection? What is the governing note of his advice? Is it to please you or to please God? Does he yield to the pull of the easy or does he try to hold you to the hard, even as our Lord set His face like a flint (Isa. 50:7) and taught His disciples to do so too?

Answer these questions honestly and your question is answered.

❖ As the leader of a community numbering at one time over nine hundred, there was constant need for vision and clear guidance and Amma often wrote about this to her family:

Fresh Vision

"Where there is no vision the people perish" (Prov. 29:18) is as true of a community of the Lord's lovers as of a nation. These words are on the wall of our Prayer Room, but that is not enough.

It has always been our custom, when in need of fresh vision about something which concerned us all, to wait in His presence till we could say "It seemed good to the Holy Spirit and to us" (Acts 15:28) to take a certain course.

First there is perhaps a long waiting in quietness for the direction of the Holy Spirit. The mind God has given us has to be used. We think, we ponder, but definitely as those who are subject to light from above. Then it has often happened that some word in Scripture has been illuminated so that it cast a light upon the matter in question.

After that has happened there is always peace, and sooner or later our God so directs circumstances that the way is opened for obedience to the light given.

Obey Your Light

Some are perplexed by diverse counsels, and yet deep within them is the word, "Obey thy light and fear it, for it is of God."

Abraham Lincoln said, "I hope it will not be irreverent for me to say that if it is probable that God would reveal His will to others on a point so connected with my duty, it might be supposed He would reveal it directly to me; for, unless I am more deceived in myself than I often am, it is my earnest desire to know the will of Providence in this matter."

There was a time when we were where Lincoln was when he said that. Often the words in John 10:3–5, about the sheep hearing the Shepherd's voice and not knowing the voice of strangers, used to help. But the difficulty was, those who gave advice with such assurance were no strangers but, we felt, much better people than we were. And yet in our hearts we knew that they had not spent as many minutes in the presence of the Lord about the matter in question as we had spent months. So how could they be so sure of His direction?

❖   Sometimes Amma followed the advice of these "much better people." Often they were right, but sometimes they were wrong, and then Amma was troubled. She wrote:

Waiting on God

It was a time of much perplexity over certain arrangements I had been advised to make, which proved unworkable. I was troubled and sorry of heart, for is there any need for those who walk with God to err in vision and stumble in judgment (Isa. 28:7)? I felt there must be a cause, and in seeking to find it came upon this: Our times of prayer together had become too hurried. We had not seen our way, because of pressure of work for the children, to wait enough on the Lord. We had prayed but not waited in that stillness which must be if we are to hear the word saying to us, "This is the way; walk in it" (Isa. 30:21).

We agreed that, cost what it might, we must have more quiet. Now, instead of prayer around the table as of old, we go to my room and shut the door (with all that word implies) and give ourselves up to stillness for half an hour or so, praying aloud if so moved, but giving as much time to listening as to speaking, and usually much more.

We have found that the work done afterwards is done in such a quietness of spirit that it is more effective than before. So time is saved, not lost. Above all, that still time seems to bring us into such a sweetness of peace, such a sense of the nearness (but nearness is too distant a word) of our dear Lord, that the whole day is sweetened by it.

Battle Guidance

"The Philistines deployed themselves in the valley of Rephaim. And David inquired of the Lord, saying, 'Shall I go up against the Philistines? Will you deliver them into my hand?' And the Lord said to David, 'Go up. . . .' Then the Philistines went up once again and deployed themselves in the valley of

Rephaim. And when David inquired of the Lord, He said, 'You shall not go up'" (2 Sam. 5:18–25, NKJV).

For each new battle there must be a new inquiry, new guidance, if there is to be victory. "As we have done, so shall we do" is not a rule in God's army. We *cannot* march until we get the Captain's marching orders. And we need not try to fight (if we do it will end in failure) until we hear the distinct "sound" (v. 24) of the Lord, for only then do we know with certainty that He is going out before us.

The Future

"Your word is a lamp to my feet and a light to my path" (Ps. 119:105, NKJV). We walk by lamplight, not by electric floodlight. We only see a few steps ahead. But we shall be shown, before we have to turn difficult corners, what we should do and how we should do it.

Nothing in the past commits us to the future except where principles are concerned. They hold. We may be shown new ways—I expect we shall. There is nothing to fear in that, if only we don't rush but serve our God with a quiet mind. He is the God of tomorrow as well as of today.

Many a dismal letter I have had about what people call "the future," and many a time I have spread such letters before the Lord and told Him that I knew He would be in the future as He had been in the past, and as He was in the present. And now it seems to me we never reach the future. By the time we come to it, it is the present.

❖   Amma's words about the future were comforting, but some who were leading the work were still troubled. "What are we to do if we have made a mistake in our guidance?" they asked. Amma's reply was typically realistic:

No Good Way Out

Are you in distress because there seems to be no good way out of a perplexing impasse?

Some years ago we were in great trouble. We had made a mistake. To get off the wrong path into the right path again meant starting an avalanche of distressing talk.

In his life of Gladstone, Morley writes: "It is one of the commonest of all secrets of cheap misjudgment in human affairs, to start by assuming that there is always some good way out of a bad case. Alas for us all, this is not so. Situations arise . . . from which no good way out exists, but only choice between a bad way and worse."

Very earnestly I would say to any who are responsible for the purity of a work, at all costs keep it pure. To do so may cost far, far more than you ever dreamed it would. Do not falter. To falter is to sap the very foundations of that which was committed to you to guard. It is to build into your city walls stones of no eternal worth. Ponder the word, "And the foundations of the city were garnished with all manner of precious stones" (Rev. 21:19), and cost what it may, resolve to build no other into your city wall.

❖ The "impasse" to which Amma referred was that she had accepted candidates who later proved to be unsuitable. Asking them to leave was one of the hardest things she was ever called upon to do, and it did indeed "start an avalanche of distressing talk."

Beautiful and Sound

When we were building our house in the Forest, I remember choosing some colored stones which the blasting of the rocks disclosed. The mason who was helping me discarded them one by one.

"But they are beautiful!" I said, not understanding.

"Beautiful, but not sound," he answered; and he took one and hammered it. "See, it crumbles. These stones will not stand pressure."

I learned much from that. The stones chosen for the building of the wall of God's pure City were beautiful jewels indeed, but they were more than beautiful. Jewels are sound. They can stand pressure.

May the Lord make us His faithful builders and keep the work He has entrusted to us a precious thing unto Himself.

Daily Leading

We ask for His leading for our day, and then we go on peacefully from unimportant-looking hour to hour, believing that it is being given, though often we do not see at the time any special sign of such guidance. Then suddenly, sometimes, it is as if there were a sudden showing, and the place that looked a mere emptiness of darkness is alight. And we know that there is not a decision taken in perplexity but looking towards Him—not an untoward circumstance (as we reckon it), not a grief, not a joy, not an innermost thought or a secret pang—but is subservient to a purpose as yet unrevealed. For we only see in part now, and how little a whisper is heard of Him.

At the end we shall see that there were no unimportant hours in life and that every minute mattered. Not a date is tumbled haphazard into our month; each date, each detail moves obedient to a Master-word unheard by us. Where we think there is only a void, there is already, only waiting to be revealed, a whole golden globeful of the purposes of God.

GOADS

❖   "The words of the wise are like goads, their collected sayings like firmly embedded nails—given by one Shepherd" (Eccles. 12:11, NIV).

Amma was aware of the many ways in which the fellowship could slip into disobedience to the light that had been given. There were many "perils" which she had experienced in her own life and in the lives of members of her family. Once she wrote down some of them. They are indeed goads— "like the sharp sticks that shepherds use to guide sheep. . . . They have been given by God, the one Shepherd of us all" (GNB).

The Peril of Irreverence

Guard all references to the Lord lest they come carelessly and do nothing. He is the Holy One as well as our beloved Savior. I fear irreverent use of His name, irreverent singing. Be very careful how you sing. Sometimes the singing of hymns and lyrics is simple blasphemy. It is taking the name of our God in vain.

That is one of the dangers of loud-shrieking singing (such as was common in some church congregations). Just as in anger, if one allows oneself to raise one's voice anger is fed, so in singing, careless shouting feeds irreverence.

There are wicked spiritual beings all about us, who, knowing the immense power for good there is in reverence, are continually quietly trying to make us forget what *they* never forget —no, not for one moment.

The Peril of Wobbling

It is written of George Fox that he was as stiff as a tree and as pure as a bell. He could not be bent by suffering of any kind to yield one inch to those who set themselves to make him yield. He always rang true to his convictions.

It is written of Moses that when first he tried to help his people he "looked this way and that way," and the end of that was flight (Exod. 2:12–15). But later things were different. Of that same man it is written, "He endured, as seeing him who is invisible" (Heb. 11:27).

Cheyne's translation of Psalm 101:3 is "Deeds that swerve do I hate."

The Peril of the Comfortable

There is a very thin razor-edge between what we should have for the sake of doing our work better, and what we should *not* have because it would enervate, soften, weaken the warrior-spirit in us. If we walk close to our Lord, who for our sakes became poor, we shall be kept from slipping on this thin edge.

Let us possess things only to share them. Let us find joy in being able to do without rather than having. Let us never, never forget that He who was rich became poor for our sakes. We follow "Poor Christ Crucified," and there were no cushions on His cross.

There is *the peril of yielding* when we foresee a difficulty which will follow as a result of obedience. With that is linked *the peril of evading the responsibility of seeking light* concerning new decisions forced upon us because of new conditions. Don't let us fear any crevasse however impossible. How shall we cross it? The Lord knows how.

The peril of turning back follows close upon *the peril of the dimmed vision.* "Where there is no vision the people perish" (Prov. 29:18). This terrible peril is never far from us. There are Powers watching in the shadows to influence our unguarded moments. King Saul of Israel, Demas, Judas—these and other names come to mind.

The most solemn words in the Bible were spoken to those who, having begun well, turn back. "But Jesus said to him, 'No one, having put his hand to the plow, and looking back, is fit for the kingdom of God'" (Luke 9:62, NKJV). "If any man draw back, my soul shall have no pleasure in him" (Heb. 10:38).

We may be betrayed into this dreadful turning back by fear: "I cannot go on to the end." There is nothing in all the world as needless as fear. From Genesis to Revelation the word rings out, *Fear not; be not afraid.* We are not the first who have been tempted to fear, and we shall not be the last. That is why this *fear not* meets us everywhere in the Book.

A thought that has helped many is this: As the mile is divided into furlongs, yards, feet, inches; as the day is divided into hours, minutes, moments; so life is divided into many little portions. Can I not trust for strength to live for the next five minutes? the next minute? this moment? I can. That is enough.

The Peril of Complacency

It is possible for one who has climbed well to settle down in a sort of smug satisfaction. When that happens he finds a comfortable rock, sits on it and surveys life comfortably. He is not set upon fresh achievements. Has he not done enough?

How am I to know if I am in this peril? If something difficult is asked of me and I shrink from it, then I may be sure I am already deep in that peril or very near it.

If I retreat before a call which a few years ago would have been a trumpet call to me, if I am content with what I have done and am not keen to achieve more, far more, then I am caught by the peril of complacency and that poorest of things, smug satisfaction.

The Peril of the Intrusion of the "I"

Someone has said that God can do anything through one who does not care whether or not he gets the credit.

If the "I" comes in at all, the work is stained and spoiled. What does it matter who suggests a thing or whose advice is followed if only the best is done? Who knows who set the stones in the arches of St. Giles Cathedral (or any beautiful building), and what does it matter, if only the building is perfect?

The Peril of Idle Words

See Matthew 12:36: "But I say to you that for every idle word men may speak, they will give account of it in the day of judgment" (NKJV). "Idle" means useless, ineffectual for good. There is a snare in talking for talking's sake. Even the simplest and apparently lightest word can be effectual for good. It may uplift a downcast heart; but aimless chatter never does, and it often slips from the merely useless to the harmful.

When a number of people meet together, there is always this peril in the offing. Mealtimes can be down-pulling, weakening; or they can be used for the kind of talk that uplifts. He who was known to His disciples in the breaking of bread is with us at mealtimes. Do we always remember that, and enjoy Him, and each other in Him?

Satan delights to tangle us in what Paul calls "foolish disputes and contentions" which are "unprofitable and useless" (Titus 3:9, NKJV).

We are here to live holy lives, clean and clear and loving; to do our daily work faithfully; to watch for our coming Lord; to win souls for Him, taking every chance we get, so that we may help everyone in every way we can.

Nothing else matters much. If each day you take some word of your Lord and by His grace set yourself to live according to that word, you will find that you have neither time for, nor interest in, tangles of profitless talk.

The Peril of Worthless Reading

Some books are worth reading; many are not. Never read a book that you would not read if you could not share it with the Lord Jesus. Some books soil the spirit; keep clear of them. Learn to discriminate as you read. There is chaff in some books in which there is also wheat; learn to separate the one from the other. Leave the chaff and take the wheat. But don't waste one minute on books that are entirely made of chaff or worse.

Few books are worth reading at all that are not worth reading twice or oftener. The Bible is the only book that will bear a lifetime's reading; one of the signs of its divine origin is that we never come to the end of its riches.

There are caterpillars whose skin is transparent. You look at them and see the food on which they feed. The skin of our souls too is transparent; looking at us, people see that on which we feed. They are helped or hindered according to the nature of that food; for no man lives to himself.

There will not be much of "the power of an endless life" about us if we feed on the sawdust of time.

The Peril of Slackness

God is patient to wait, but I think we sometimes try to use His patience as a cover for our slackness. His is no easy patience; He is patient but He is ardent. There is something awful in His ardor. "God so loved that He gave." Are we so loving that we are giving? How are we giving? Without limit, without pause? The time may be short.

The Peril of Evading Responsibility

"In the morning will I direct my prayer unto thee, and will look up" (Ps. 5:3).

Do all who come together for prayer take their full share, or do some slip the responsibility on to the leaders?

The verb in Psalm 5:3 is a priestly word. It was used to describe the priest's work in arranging the sacrifice, and if we are Christians we are "a holy priesthood, to offer up spiritual sacrifices" (1 Pet. 2:5, NKJV). So this word is for us all and we mustn't say someone else is responsible for the meeting and leave it at that. Each one is meant to share by coming prepared in spirit, and by careful thought over what is to be prayed for, that it may be set before the Lord.

What a difference it makes if there is this preparation and all come truly ready! Five minutes of such prayer is worth more than hours of the ordinary kind.

God make us all "helpers together" in prayer.

The Peril of Failing to Hold a Soul to the Highest

When the Lord gives a command to a soul (and there is always a promise attached to a command), at first the soul is bathed in joy. But soon it goes down into darkness. It is swept by storms, broken and dismayed. "Until the time that [Joseph's] word came to pass, the word of the Lord tested him" (Ps. 105:19, NKJV). To be tested is not easy; it can be a terrific experience.

If a friend alongside, knowing something of this matter and longing to ease the situation, persuades the one to whom the command was given that it must have been a mistake; or that he need not go quite all the way in obedience—then that friend falls into this peril.

Nothing so surely proves true love as does steadfast faithfulness in holding a loved one to the highest.

The Peril of Lowering His Standard

God wants not only courage and strength, He wants the sweetness of sweet incense too. This is illustrated in the directions He gave about the pure incense, which shows our Lord Jesus Christ. All the ingredients were useful, except calamus. It had no use except that of sweetness. Was this to teach us that just to be sweet-tempered matters? (Exod. 30:34–36).

No special quantity was named because the graces of our Lord had no limit; but each spice used had to be of equal amount, because "no one quality ever displaced or interfered with the other."

All was beaten very small, because "every little movement in the life of Christ, every minute circumstance, every trait," gives forth a perfume produced by "a like-weight of all the divine graces that compose His character."

And as He is, so are we in this world (1 John 4:17). There is provision that it may be so. We are called to walk just as He walked (1 John 2:6).

"Too high a standard"? It is His, not ours. Dare we lower it? God forgive us if we have lowered it.

Basket

11

En Route for Heaven

❖ Heaven is very real to all members of the Dohnavur family. Death holds no fears for them, for "to depart and be with Christ, which is far better" (Phil. 1:23) is not a pious platitude but a truth they have imbibed from their infancy. Young or old, they look forward to heaven as the greatest possible joy. When anyone is told she is not likely to recover from her illness, her reaction is excitement and delight.

It was of course Amma who inspired this attitude, and she once wrote to her family about it:

Death

There are two ways of looking at death: the pagan way and the Christian way. Many Christians, without meaning to do so, look at death in the pagan way. When my father died we all wore black for two years and wrote on notepaper edged with black. When people spoke of him they said, "Your poor father."

When my mother passed on we made the Praise Room bright with lights and beautiful with flowers. You all stood in the dark courtyard and then came into the shining room, and we sang together the most heavenly hymns we knew and were happy in her happiness.

The pagan way of looking at death is full of sadness; the Christian way is full of gladness. Our Lord described it when He said, "If you loved Me you would rejoice because I said, 'I am going to the Father'" (John 14:28, NKJV).

I suppose as we pass through the waters of death, or as we rise through the quickening air, all that would sadden in memory will fade from our minds, and all the joyful blessed things will stand out, each one shining as the stars shine in the blue of an Eastern night. How wonderful it will be, to be able to turn the pages back and see how excellent were those ways of His, of which down here we heard so little a whisper.

Rise, He Calls

Ten days ago C.H. said to his wife, "I have had no dream or vision, and yet I feel that I am going soon to God. I want you to be baptized now, so that we may be one in our Christian confession."

His wish was fulfilled (she too is a true believer), and then the very next day, "Be of good cheer: rise, he calleth thee. And he, casting away his garment, sprang up, and came to Jesus" (Mark 10:49–50, RV).

I do so delight in this Revised Version rendering, "sprang up." It sounds so eager. And I love also the quick casting away of the garments. If our Lord tarries, that is what we shall gladly do when, like the pilgrims, we leave our mortal garments behind us in the river, as we read in *Pilgrim's Progress*.

Surely joy-bells should be rung—not bells tolled—when a pilgrim is met by the Shining Ones and goes up through the regions of air.

❖ And in Dohnavur joy-bells *are* rung as soon as one of the family goes to be with the Lord. A hymn tune is played on the tubular bells, and though there is the sadness of loss, the predominant thought is joy and praise.

Although heaven was so real to her, Amma felt the grief and loss of bereavement as deeply as anyone else. In the early days many of the babies, saved after much prayer and cared for so devotedly, slipped away in the end, leaving Amma and her helpers grieving. She never grew used to it. Each baby was a precious individual, and Amma loved as only a mother can.

But as usual her own sense of loss and grief made her think of others in similar distress, and she sought to share her comfort with them in her letters.

The Death of a Baby

This may reach someone who has lately lent a treasure to the Lord of love. I say *lent* because I believe we do not "render Him with patience what He lent" (as Milton wrote "On a fair infant dying of a cough"). We *lend Him what He gave*.

Hannah chose her verbs rightly: "For this child I prayed, and the Lord has granted me my petition which I asked of Him. Therefore I also have lent him to the Lord" (1 Sam. 1:27–28, NKJV). I pin my faith to these two scriptures: Romans 11:29 (NKJV), "The gifts of God are irrevocable" ("God never goes back on a gift" is one rendering of that) and James 1:17 (NKJV), "Every good gift and every perfect gift"—is not a little child just that?— "is from above, and comes down from the Father of lights, with whom is no variation or shadow of turning."

Surely our Father is more father-like than some would have us think. In a little while our treasure will be given back to us more "good and perfect" than we can imagine now. Our loans do not lose in beauty during the little while they are lent.

Dear Master, all the flowers are Thine,
And false the whisper, "ours" and "mine."
We lift our hearts to Thee and say:
"Lord, it was Thine to take away."

And yet, though we would have it so,
Lord, it is very good to know
That Thou art feeling for our pain;
And we shall have our flower again.

So help us now to be content
To take the sorrow Thou hast sent.
Dear Lord, how fair Thy house must be
With all the flowers we've lent to Thee!

❖ Amma had many opportunities to practice what she
taught. One after the other throughout her lifetime, those
she counted on for the leadership of the work which was more
dear to her than anything else, were taken away.

The first to go was Mr. Walker (whose life she wrote in
This One Thing). He was not only her senior missionary; he
was her friend and adviser, and gave the help she sorely needed
in the beginning of the work to save children. His death was
sudden and unexpected. Everyone knew what a blow it was
to Amma.

Mr. Walker's Death

Ponnammal knew what Mr. Walker had been to me; she
knew I would be feeling just bereft. She comforted me, telling
me now God would be more to me than ever, for He knew I
had no arm but His, no help but in Himself.

Today she came with a new thought. "I believe there is a

secret in this matter. God knew he was a could-not-be-done-without one. And yet God said, 'Do without.' There is a secret in it."

A secret—it does not matter whether or not it is explained. "What I am doing you do not understand now, but you will know after this" (John 13:7, NKJV) is a most loving word. But I sometimes feel it will be just as perfect whether or not it is explained, because we know our Father, so we know His secrets cannot possibly contain anything but love.

Rejoice in the Lord

Sometimes letters come which, however kind in purpose, do not strike me as at all true in view.

"It is very hard to see how this can be for the best." But we are not asked to see, and why need we, when we KNOW?

"It is such an irreparable loss that it is very hard to trust all is for the best." Truly it is an irreparable loss, but is it faith at all if it is "hard to trust" when things are entirely bewildering?

There is something in this kind of talk which makes me feel like sympathizing with the Father who hears it. He must feel a little as I would if I heard two of my children discussing something I had done and finishing up with, "It is very hard to trust her." For really isn't that what such talk comes to? Oh, let us have done with it!

The pain of parting and the sense of missing does not pass; it seems to get keener. But is not that pain quite different from the attitude of soul which gives color to the impression that our God has been a little less loving than usual, a little hard; or else that somehow He has made a mistake?

So let us glorify Him and rejoice His heart by trusting Him

and living as those who really and truly do believe that this which He has chosen is the very best, most loving, and afterwards is to end in the most joyful choice He could have made for us.

It is easy to write this, but may God save us from "paper grace" and give us grace to live it, and to continue to live it!

"As a help in distress He is thoroughly proved" is Delitzsch's translation of Psalm 46:1. From the very depths of our sorrow and sore sense of loss and need, I do want to say, Rejoice with us!

"Yet will I rejoice in the Lord" (Hab. 3:18).

"I have more than an overweight of joy" (2 Cor. 7:4, Conybeare's translation).

Our joy is set in the Lord, not in happy circumstances, not even in human friendship and fellowship and comradeship. However the sorrow side of the scale is weighed down today, it is true, thank God it is true, we have more than an overweight of joy.

"Let your hope be something exultant: in affliction never flinch," is Way's beautiful translation of Romans 12:12.

❖ In 1899 a little girl of eleven heard the gospel for the first time when Amma and her band were preaching in her village. Amma tells her story in *Ploughed Under*. By a series of miracles, Arulai was allowed to join Amma and became her "treasure child," the one she loved most on earth. She had unique gifts and was as totally committed to the Lord as Amma, and Amma and all the family expected her to become leader of the women and girls when Amma passed on.

But she was delicate; several times she nearly died, but the Lord healed her in answer to prayer. In 1939, after months of illness, it was she who went first to be with the Lord. There had been constant prayer for her healing, and Amma never gave up hope even when it was clear that all human hope had gone.

A note written to her family the morning after Arulai's death shows how she reacted:

Arulai

It has been my custom to spend my first waking moments with God for you all. This morning instead of that I found myself thinking of Arulai, longing for her, longing to know what she is doing—such vain longings.

Suddenly I realized that I was spending these minutes in something that would help nobody. I was wasting minutes that would never return. And I began to think of all the treasures left to me. Face by face I thought of you and thanked God for you, and felt how ungrateful it was to spend time that belonged to you in this way, this useless way.

Some of you who love Arulai very dearly may be tempted as I was this morning. If you are, turn from that temptation and think of the treasures our God has left to us.

❖ Amma was accustomed to finding her help in the Bible, and Delitzsch's notes on Psalm 42 were both a challenge and a comfort to her. She wrote:

Why Sad?

"Why am I so sad? Why am I so troubled? I will put my hope in God, and once again I will praise Him, my Savior and my God" (Ps. 42:5, Delitzsch).

Why? Here the spirit, the stronger and more valiant part of

the man, speaks to the soul. It is good to call the weak soul to account and to brace it to courage by turning it from itself and its grief to God Himself and His eternal verities. At the longest, how very brief our grief will be. There is nothing eternal in this sorrow (this bereavement)—nothing bitter. Do not let us even for a moment sorrow as those who have no hope, no sweetness in their grief.

> Dear Lord, to Thee I pray,
>   Make me a very simple child,
> No fancies wild and no exaggeration of the way
>   I go today.

Why this gnawing, despondent grief? I shall yet praise Him.

And yet—verses 6 and 7: "My heart is breaking, and so turn my thoughts to Him. He has sent waves of sorrow over my soul."

This is true to life. There is no pretence in the sacred writings, no posing. But the soul does not abandon itself to grief. There is an effort to remember the source of its strength. "Within me my soul is cast down . . . *therefore* do I remember Thee" (Delitzsch).

❖   Amma always tried to see and comfort anyone who was in trouble, and she was often encouraged herself by the stories they had to tell which showed the Lord's love. She shared with her friends overseas the stories of two male converts:

Paradesie

Paradesie's wife died in Neyoor a few months ago. The day she died, as he was walking up and down the Neyoor street in great trouble, the wind blew a bit of paper across his shoulder. He caught it and was about to throw it away when he saw printing on it. It was a scrap from a book, and on it were just these words:

> I have finished my race.
> I sought to be a faithful wife.
> I have received consolation.

It was enough. Fortified and comforted, he went back to the young dying mother and the three little children and never for one moment did he break down.

"How could I fear when God had sent the wind to blow His comfort to me?"

Cornelius

After his conversion Cornelius witnessed to all his neighbors, much to the disgust of his first-born son who was old enough to feel the stigma, and who protested vigorously. Then this son became very ill, but before he died "his heart was touched and was turned and he was changed," Cornelius says.

On the day of his death he said to his father, "I shall go to the heavenly city today." Then as the household gathered around him he said, "Is there anything I should do before I go?"

"Yes," said Cornelius, "I think you should apologize for all your tongue said when I witnessed of the Lord's salvation to my neighbors."

The boy immediately joined his hands together in the Indian way and humbly asked each one present for pardon. After this he died.

The villagers came in the usual way to mourn and condole, but Cornelius said, "No, let us make a feast." He had coffee made for them and gave them fruit.

After this the valiant Cornelius went to a neighboring vil-

lage to pray for the recovery of a little boy who was ill. As he
returned home, crossing the open plain, he saw, he says, his
own dear boy, his first-born, "being carried up in light." He
says nothing of how he was carried—he did not notice that—
only that he was sure he was given a glimpse of his happy son.
"He looked different, but I know that it was he. He looked
very, very happy."

It is like India to tell a story like this in the most ordinary
simple way, thinking nothing of it really, except that it was comforting.

Heaven

What must heaven keep in store for us if earth can offer us
such unimaginable beauty?

I have a tiny blue feather, so unbelievably blue that you feel
as you look at it that only God could have thought of such a
blue. I wonder what heaven will have for us in the way of sur-
prises of color? Did you ever think how impossible it is to imagine a new color, and yet the Creator of color is not confined to
seven and combinations of seven.

What dazzling mysteries lie just beyond our view! I do not
wonder that men who were given glimpses of these glories fell
back on similitudes and the phrase *as it were*. "As it were a paved
work of sapphire stone; and as it were the body of heaven in his
clearness" (Exod. 24:10).

But it will be love that makes heaven. Beauty alone would
leave us cold. Think what it will be to look around and not see
a single unloving face, and to know that in all heaven there is
not one who can think an unkind thought.

Among our little children we often find such a generous

affection that I think it must be part of their heavenly heritage, which they have not had time to lose.

Travelers' Joy

All men travel. Some find travelers' joy.* When we consider the home to which we travel, the condition of the road does not seem to matter so much. There are only a few more miles, and in the hedges travelers' joy is growing. One day the road will lead into something too wonderful and delightful to be described by words of man—deliverance from the bondage of corruption into the glorious liberty of the children of God (Rom. 8:21).

Meantime—"Roll thy way upon the Lord" (Ps. 37:5, RV margin). "Leave the guidance of your life entirely to Him, and to Him alone. He will gloriously accomplish all that concerns thee" is Delitzsch's paraphrase of the verse.

"Rest in the Lord, and wait patiently for him" (Ps. 37:7). The Hebrew word translated "wait" means "to strengthen oneself to endure, continue; expect to be on the stretch, yet without strain."

God help us to learn this lesson so well that He may soon be able to turn the page. What will its lesson be? And what will it be when the last page is turned, the last lesson learned that will ever be blotted by tears on the book? Oh, what will it be when the book is closed and a new glorious lesson book opened, and we look up and see a Face? O perfect, patient heavenly Teacher of dull and slow and heavy learners—what will it be to see You face to face?

---

* An ornamental climbing plant with fragrant green-white flowers.

Basket

12

Triumph!

❖ "For he must reign till he has put all enemies under his feet. The last enemy that will be destroyed is death" (1 Cor. 15:25–26).

He must reign—that was the whole purpose of Amma's life and writings, so this last basket shall contain her account of one wonderful instance of His victory over death and the fear of death.

Not Tragedy—Triumph

The first we heard of Jebamonie was what a scrawled postcard told: It said he was in jail, about to be tried for killing his wife, and would we shelter his three little children?

I sent this postcard to a friend, asking her to find out what she could about Jebamonie as she lives opposite the jail. She did, and I could see from her letter that she felt much for him. His wife had been wicked; he had tried to reform her but in vain. At last, in a sudden passion, he had killed her.

He meant to kill himself also (this he told me when I saw him) but had suddenly remembered his poor little children, for whom he felt he must make some safe arrangement. He gave himself up, told all he had done and was of course remanded for trial.

On his way to jail, being in the depths of despair, he had been comforted by a magistrate. "Do not break your heart over that," said the magistrate, and told him to write to us.

Alec took me to the jail, and we found the Superintendent and the jailers were feeling much for Jebamonie. He had just been condemned to death. There had been three jurymen: two found the crime manslaughter, one found it murder. The judge held with the one who found it murder and sentenced him accordingly.

So I was taken to the condemned cell, a small strongly-barred place set within an enclosure by itself. It was hard to talk to him through bars, and the jailer was very kind and let me in and locked me up with him. He spread his mat on the floor and we sat on it together and he told me his story.

To such a man, such a crime is hardly a crime. None of the people in the village, where all is known, blame him in the least. He was what is called here "a born Christian," and this may mean very little. He had no feeling at all beyond a vague and general sense of having done something better left undone.

His mind was not on himself but on his children, so the first thing was to relieve his mind about them. At last, this settled, it was possible to get him to consider his own tremendous need. After a long time—to my relief the jailer did not hurry us—he did, as I believe, turn to the Lord in true penitence and faith. And then suddenly he looked up.

"Now it does not matter if they hang me on the hanging tree!" he laughed. And I laughed too, for joy. No, indeed it did not matter if they hanged him; nothing mattered now.

The guard outside the bars looked in, astonished. I wonder if they had ever heard laughter in that cell before. The jailer and

Alec turned around too; it was an astonishing moment.

Although I had found him indifferent in one way, in another way he had seemed strangely prepared in spirit; and I wondered over this, till in the simple way of the Tamil he told me how, early that morning, he had a dream. One, he did not know who it was, came to him and gave him a Bible.

"I had been longing for a Bible. In my house there is a Bible and a New Testament and a lyric book. But I had nothing here."

Think of the long dreadful weeks between crime and trial, and the age-long five days after the sentence, and nothing to do, nothing to read. I wonder such a man does not go mad.

"But from that dream," said Jebamonie with a swift, beaming smile, "I knew something good was appointed for today."

"You shall have that Bible today," I said. So his dream was fulfilled.

❖ On Saturday about three months later, Amma was again in the jail. Jebamonie's appeal to the High Court had failed; he then had appealed to the Governor and, as that failed, to the Viceroy. There was little hope of a pardon, and in that case the execution would be at dawn on Wednesday. But Amma continued:

It was a wonderful time. After a little while with Jebamonie, I went on to the next cell, and the next, forgetting in my pity for those poor hopeless men that Christians may only speak to Christians. Presently I heard the head jailer saying something about the fuss the public would make if there were conversions in the jail, and I stopped. It is not fair to break the rules which are not of the jailers' making and which they must obey.

It was sad to leave the men comfortless. But as I turned reluctantly from the miserable face of the man in the cell next to Jebamonie he said, "I never heard before of your Lord Jesus, but I am hearing now. The prisoner in the next cell talks continually to Him and reads aloud from His book."

So the merciful Lord had His way of reaching those men after all. Several down that dreary line must have heard. Jebamonie's voice carried well, and his jailers were good to him; they did not silence him.

There he stood as we turned to go, content; his Bible under one arm, his New Testament under the other. Inside their covers he had pasted (probably with a pickle of rice) a letter of mine quoting 1 John 1:8–9, John 6:37, and that ever-beloved passage Isaiah 41:10, which I had written out in full.

We left him, feeling more than ever that our God's name is *Wonderful.*

"He is here; He is shining in my cell," Jebamonie had said as he held my hands in his between the bars. I looked into the desolate place. The cell was bare to the eye of flesh, but how little of what *is* do we see. That joyful face under its white jail cap, that peace, with the rope just four days away—no one who saw it will ever forget.

We left home at 3:30 a.m. on Wednesday. For a while we waited outside the jail gates in the bright moonlight. Then the head jailer came.

"It may make him nervous at the end if he sees you," he said.

But the family at home was in prayer. We were asking a great thing from our God, even perfect peace, and we told him that to see us would not make Jebamonie nervous.

He disappeared however into the yawning mouth of the jail, leaving us still outside. When one remembers what it must be like when a man who is going to be hanged is "nervous," one cannot wonder that the jailer was not anxious to take risks.

Presently the Superintendent came. He looked strained; this execution evidently was not a trifle to him, nor to the head jailer who had to do it. They had to do their duty but they were humane men, and the thing must have felt intolerable. They knew of the fierce provocation of that unfaithful wife.

The Superintendent did not seem to fear he would be "nervous." He took me straight to the enclosure where the row of condemned cells are. Jebamonie was standing in his clean white jail cap, tunic and shorts, surrounded by his guards, in front of his cell. His arms were roped behind his back. His face seen in full moonlight was radiant. "Amma, salaam"—involuntarily he tried to raise his bound hands, but the peace on his face was not shaken. He turned upon me a beaming smile of welcome.

"This is a good day for you, dear Jebamonie. You will see our Lord Jesus today."

"Yes, I shall see our Lord Jesus. Very soon I shall see Him!"

For a minute we were both silent; a sort of exultant silence held us. The Superintendent was silent, gazing at Jebamonie. The guards gazed at him too; from the long row of condemned cells eyes were watching from behind the bars.

Then Jebamonie burst forth into praise. That voice of his, so strong and vibrant that it was impossible to think of it stilled within fifteen minutes, ran down the line of cells and out far across the enclosure.

"If we say that we have no sin we deceive ourselves, and the truth is not in us. If we confess our sins He is faithful and just to forgive us our sins and thoroughly to cleanse us from all unrighteousness. Surely He hath borne Jebamonie's griefs, and carried Jebamonie's sorrows. He was wounded for Jebamonie's transgressions. He was bruised for Jebamonie's iniquities. The anguish that causes peace to be for Jebamonie, that anguish fell upon Him."

Without a pause those words flowed forth. The eight condemned men in their cells must have heard them all.

Then, looking up into the moonlit sky, Jebamonie began again: "Fear thou not, for I am with thee; be not dismayed, for I am thy God: I will strengthen thee, yea I will help thee, yea I will uphold thee with the right hand of My righteousness."

Another pause. Still the Superintendent waited, his official book and papers under his arm, his eyes on Jebamonie's face.

"My Lord and Savior Jesus Christ spoke these words, *'Him that cometh to Me I will in no wise cast out.'* To me has been given the forgiveness of sins through my Lord Jesus Christ.

"Bless the Lord, O my soul: and all that is within me, bless His holy name.

"Bless the Lord, O my soul, and forget not all His benefits: who forgiveth all thine iniquities: who healeth all thy diseases: who redeemeth thy life from destruction: who crowneth thee with loving-kindness and tender mercies."

Then in one swift stream poured forth verse after verse from many different psalms, verses of adoration and thanksgiving. It was a victory of the grace of God that passed, far passed, our bravest prayers. We had asked for peace, for courage to the end. This glory of adoration was something exceeding abundant, above what we had asked or thought.

"Blessed be the Lord because He hath heard the voice of my supplications. The Lord is my strength and my shield, my heart trusted in Him and I am helped, therefore my heart greatly rejoiceth and with my song will I praise Him. The Lord is my Shepherd. I shall not want. Yea, though I walk through the valley of the shadow of death I will fear no evil, for Thou art with me. Thy rod and Thy staff, they comfort me. Surely goodness and mercy shall follow me all the days of my life and I will dwell in the house of the Lord forever."

The Superintendent did not want to interrupt him; I think he felt it as sacred as I did. But in the east there was a hint of rose and I saw him glance at his watch. Jebamonie stopped. "Glory be to the Father and to the Son and to the Holy Ghost. As it was in the beginning, is now, and ever shall be. Amen," he said, and waited.

Then I prayed—rather, I too worshiped and adored. What was there left to ask?

He told me how he trusted his children to me, and I promised to mother them. Then the Superintendent did his obnoxious duty, touching a mark of identification in Jebamonie's neck, reading out of a huge book that crime that was washed out of remembrance in the Books of Eternity, producing the futile appeals, great sheets of formal writing. I saw poor Jebamonie's rapt look break for just one moment; it was as though he were being pulled back to earth, and I sent up one swift cry for help.

With a sigh as if of relief the Superintendent shut his great book of condemnation—and once more we looked up into the pure sky and spoke to Him who was nearer than that.

Jebamonie's guards closed round him, but like all the jail people they were awed and tender, and I was allowed to be next to him. And his face was as the face of one who is walking towards the sunrising.

Suddenly he burst into a song of praise and adoration to Jesus. It was an amazing thing to hear; no one stopped him. Once he broke off—

"What is 'Bless the Lord, O my soul' in English?"

The Superintendent, much moved, answered before I could: "Sing it in Tamil, man, your God understands Tamil."

Jebamonie sang as the gate opened; the guards outside with their fixed bayonets did not draw his eyes off. I do not think he knew when I left him. He had God.

Ronald, who had waited outside the jail praying for Jebamonie while I was with him, shall tell the next:

> The time rushed by and we knew that at any moment Jebamonie would be brought out of the massive prison door and led to the execution enclosure just a few yards away. Presently we heard the sound of joyous singing, and out came Jebamonie with Amma, her hand resting on his shoulder and a crowd of warders surrounding them.
>
> It was a sight of infinite pathos, yet of such complete victory to see this man, being taken to his death, the death of a common criminal, with praise and adoration to God just pouring out of his lips. His voice never quavered.
>
> Amma, Alec and I joined in silent prayer for him who was just about to be hurled into eternity. The singing continued for a few moments; it was the only sound that disturbed the quietness of the crimson dawn.
>
> Suddenly a silence fell—we heard a sound as of a bolt being shot in a door—silence once more till we woke to the realization that it was all over, that dear Jebamonie was in glory.
>
> They came and told us how he died: singing right up till the last moment without a trace of fear. He only stopped singing when the rope was placed round his neck. He died praying.

We came back an hour later to lay his body to rest. While we waited in the office of the jail till things were ready, the officials talked to us about him. They told us that when he came in he was so desperate that the warders feared to go near him. It was evident that they had marveled at the change in him.

They told us of the peaceful way he received the news (that the last appeal had failed). "When is it to be?" he asked, and went on quietly reading.

He had sung from four o'clock that morning; he had sung continually during the day before.

"I asked him to sing to me," said the head jailer, "I liked so much to hear him."

"What did he sing?" we asked.

"Oh, praises to Jesus, and something about Emmanuel—the word came often."

Emmanuel. It reminded us of what he had said, "*God is with me here; He is shining in my cell.*"

But he had wanted his human friends and had often asked if we would come. As he stood there waiting, his last quarter of an hour begun, he had said to the deputy jailer who was with him, "She will come."

"How do you know?" said the jailer.

"I have been asking my God to send her," he said.

Just then he saw me coming. He turned to the jailer and said, "There she is!" and, his last wish granted, he greeted me with that radiant smile.

But I am glad I did not come before, for no one could say that it was any human influence that was supporting him. He had learned to lean on the arm of God.

Later on, as we looked at the peaceful face, we marveled. There was no pain in it, no fear, nothing of that dreadful snarl the jail people told us is on the face of a man who dies in terror —as many die. The mouth was half smiling; the spirit had left its impression in the flash of its passing.

Then we followed them as they carried him to the grave-yard, and once more we were allowed to bear witness to Jesus, the Lord of life and death.

We left all that could perish of Jebamonie there, on the wide plain under the wide sky, and we knew we had seen death swallowed up in victory! It was not tragedy. It was triumph. Alleluia! Amen.

Epilogue

Were Amma's prayers answered, her vision fulfilled?

Her work in India began in the villages, where she traveled around with her evangelistic band and agonized in prayer both for the nominal Christians and the unconverted millions. From that very area in South India have come a number of Christians on fire for the Lord, who are serving Him as missionaries in almost every state in India. Two men from the village which was Amma's headquarters before she moved to Dohnavur have founded two of the keenest indigenous missionary societies, with many active members.

In Dohnavur her aim was to train her boys and girls to be missionaries to their own people. That is still the aim of those who work there today, in what Amma once described as "a Garden Village." (Visitors are often surprised by the size and complexity of the place.)

In a private letter Amma wrote about a newly married girl: "I do trust that she will be a good wife and a true Christian. Sometimes my heart is sad as I think of any child redeemed at such cost, and so dearly loved, and trained so carefully, becoming an ordinary Christian: *cool*, not *burning* in her love to her Redeemer."

Many, but not all, of those brought up in Dohnavur would rejoice Amma's heart; for they are "burning" in their love and are serving the Lord as pastors, evangelists, teachers, medical workers, and in almost every imaginable walk of life in many parts of India and elsewhere. Others are "cool"; and a few (including some in Dohnavur) are as yet unconverted.

The leadership in Dohnavur is now almost entirely Indian. Children continue to be saved from abuse, exploitation or even death, and are lovingly brought up and trained in a family, not an institution. Evangelistic work, through the hospital, village outposts, meetings and house-to-house visiting, still remains a priority; and many from the surrounding villages have been won for the Lord.

For some years boys, for whom there are now other Christian homes in the area, have not been admitted. The last boys left in 1984 after completing their education. The premises they used to occupy are now filled primarily by the children of Indian missionaries, who attend a boarding school opened in 1982 by the Santhosha Educational Society. Its committee of eleven includes six members of the fellowship. There are already over 200 Indian boys and girls in this Christian school, another outreach which is surely an answer to Amma's prayers.

A success story? By no means. India's teeming millions are still largely unreached. Less than four percent of over 770 *million* souls, for whom Christ died, are even nominally Christian. The task ahead is immense.

Will *you* help?

Headquarters in India
The Dohnavur Fellowship
Dohnavur
Tirunelveli District
Tamil Nadu 627 102
India

Office in England
The Dohnavur Fellowship
380 Windmill Road
Brentford
Middlesex TW8 0QH
U.K.

This book was produced by CLC Publications. We hope it has been life-changing and has given you a fresh experience of God through the work of the Holy Spirit. CLC Publications is an outreach of CLC Ministries International, a global literature mission with work in over 50 countries. If you would like to know more about us or are interested in opportunities to serve with a faith mission, we invite you to contact us at:

CLC Ministries International
PO Box 1449
Fort Washington, PA 19034

Phone: (215) 542-1242
E-mail: clcmail@clcusa.org
Website: www.clcusa.org

- -

DO YOU LOVE GOOD CHRISTIAN BOOKS?
Do you have a heart for worldwide missions?

You can receive a FREE subscription to
CLC's newsletter on global literature missions
Order by e-mail at:

clcheartbeat@clcusa.org
or fill in the coupon below and mail to:

**P.O. Box 1449
Fort Washington, PA 19034**

FREE *HEARTBEAT* SUBSCRIPTION!

Name: _____

Address: _____

_____

Phone: _____ E-mail: _____

READ THE REMARKABLE STORY OF

the founding of
CLC International

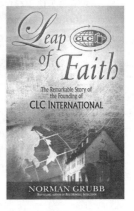

"Any who doubt that Elijah's God still lives ought to read of the money supplied when needed, the stores and houses provided, and the appearance of personnel in answer to prayer."
—Moody Monthly

Is it possible that the printing press, the editor's desk, the Christian bookstore, and the mail order department, can glow with the fast-moving drama of an "Acts of the Apostles"?

Find out, as you are carried from two people in an upstairs bookroom to a worldwide chain of Christian bookcenters, multiplied by nothing but a "shoestring" of faith and committed, though unlikely, lives.

IF

Amy Carmichael

What do I know of Calvary Love?

Based on Corinthians 13, this booklet will help you meditate on God's love and become a channel through which God can disburse His love in the world.

Mass Market ISBN 978-0-87508-071-0

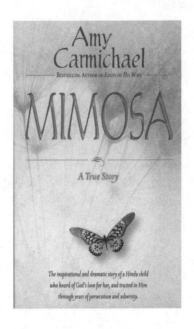

MIMOSA

Amy Carmichael

The inspiring, beautifully written true story of Mimosa, a Hindu child who heard of a God who loved her, and lived from then on under His influence, surmounting every kind of opposition and adversity.

Trade Paper ISBN 978-0-87508-821-1

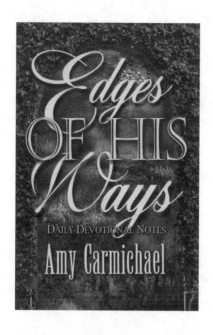

EDGES OF HIS WAYS

Amy Carmichael

Experience greater depths of God's love, compassion and intimate fellowship through this daily devotional, compiled from the writing of Amy Carmichael. **An ideal gift book.**

Trade Paper ISBN 978-0-87508-062-8

MOUNTAIN BREEZES

Amy Carmichael

An anthology of Amy Carmichael's best-loved poems, gathered from 29 of her books. **A treasure for poetry lovers.**

Trade Paper ISBN 978-0-87508-789-4
Cloth ISBN 978-0-87508-790-0

KOHILA

Amy Carmichael

The story of Kohila, who arrived at Dohnavur Fellowship at the age of four, learned the meaning of true love, and offered up her life to serve her Lord as a nurse.

Trade Paper ISBN 978-0-87508-770-7